Andrea Biondi

The Schrems rulings and the new model contract clauses.

Andrea Biondi

The Schrems rulings and the new model contract clauses.

The transfer of personal data to third countries

ScienciaScripts

Cover image: www.ingimage.com

This book is a translation from the original published under ISBN 978-3-330-77654-8.

Publisher:
Sciencia Scripts
is a trademark of
Dodo Books Indian Ocean Ltd. and OmniScriptum S.R.L publishing group

120 High Road, East Finchley, London, N2 9ED, United Kingdom
Str. Armeneasca 28/1, office 1, Chisinau MD-2012, Republic of Moldova, Europe
Printed at: see last page
ISBN: 978-620-6-28936-4

CONTENT

Privacy is from the very beginning connected to modern forms of communication and originated as a right of the golden age of the bourgeoisie, which constructed its own private space surrounded by defenses, just as it had constructed its physical space with the right to property.

With databases, networks, cable TV, and even genetic technologies-which are largely collections of information about people-the right of privacy is no longer just to be left alone, but also, and more importantly, to control the fate of the information circulating about oneself.[1]

Stefano Rodotà

---

[1] Stefano Rodotà, Technologies and Rights, Il Mulino, Bologna, 1995,
https://www.mulino.it/isbn/9788815048554
(permanent copy https://perma.cc/7Z22-ZZ4M)
cited in Teresa Serrao, Right to Privacy, la Repubblica, 1995,
https://ricerca.repubblica.it/repubblica/archivio/repubblica/1995/05/14/diritto-di-privacy.html
(permanent copy https://perma.cc/6BF3-J8HJ)

Chapter 1.
Introduction

The Schrems rulings are two measures, adopted by the Court of Justice of the European Union, regarding international agreements between Europe and the United States of America on the transfer of personal data of European citizens.

The two rulings are named after Austrian activist Maximilian Schrems who, in 2013, filed a complaint against *hi-tech* giant Facebook in connection with the way in which it processed the personal data of its users. As detailed in 0, the first Schrems ruling in 2015 leads to the invalidation of an international agreement in place since 2000 between Europe and the United States of America for the overseas transfer of personal data of European citizens.

In 2016, Europe and the United States of America then approve a new international agreement for the transfer of personal data of European citizens. In 2018, against a regulatory backdrop of the new *GDPR*, the *Irish High Court* submits eleven interpretive questions to the Court of Justice of the European Union in response to yet another complaint filed by Maximilian Schrems. As detailed in 0, the second ruling in 2020 leads to the invalidation of the new international agreement.

The two Schrems rulings, in addition to their obvious impact on the transfer of personal data overseas, also have political significance and should become an occasion for reflection: the rapid pace of technological change and globalization have demonstrated the importance of ensuring the European Union's technological and digital sovereignty; the storage and processing of data within European borders can become a lever for choosing European providers over U.S. operators for whom the necessary requirements would make overseas transfer disadvantageous.

Maximilian Schrems

Maximilian Schrems, more commonly known as Max Schrems[2], was born in Salzburg, Austria, in 1987. While studying law at the University of Vienna in 2011, Schrems had the opportunity to spend a semester abroad at Santa Clara University, Silicon Valley in the United States of America. Attending a press conference given by Edward Palmieri[3], Facebook's privacy representative, he is able to note the lack of sensitivity with respect to the issue of personal data protection and decides to focus his thesis on the *social network*'s apparent failure to understand and enforce the restrictions in European data protection legislation. In the course of his research, he learns of dossiers that include numerous pieces of personal information including information that users believe they have deleted from the *social network*.

After finishing his semester abroad and returning to Austria, Schrems founded the activist group, Europe v. Facebook[4]. The presence of a Facebook office in Ireland makes the company vulnerable to local legislation regarding the processing of personal data and, more specifically, in relation to the right of access[5] which allows every European citizen to be able to request and obtain all personal information about him or her held by a company. Schrems decides to exercise this right[6] and a few weeks later, in the summer of 2011, he receives some *CDs* by regular mail from the Facebook Inc. offices in California. He manages to ascertain that, in just three years of his personal *account*, the *social network* has collected 1,200 pages of information regarding contacts, events to which he was also simply invited, reactions to posts, access to the platform and messages, including some marked as "deleted." The report also includes information about other *accounts* of users who used the same devices as him to

---

2 Wikipedia, Max Schrems,
https://en.wikipedia.org/wiki/Max_Schrems
(permanent copy https://perma.cc/Q6KH-7YSH)

3 LinkedIn, Edward Palmieri,
https://www.linkedin.com/in/ejpalmieri/
(permanent copy https://perma.cc/VA94-UA3C)
Engineering at Meta, Edward Palmieri,
https://engineering.fb.com/author/edward-palmieri/
(permanent copy https://perma.cc/U2GX-ESXA)

4 Europe v. Facebook,
http://www.europe-v-facebook.org/EN/en.html
(permanent copy https://perma.cc/33BU-TERE)

5 Data Protection Act 1988, Right of access,
https://revisedacts.lawreform.ie/eli/1988/act/25/section/4/revised/en/html
(permanent copy *https://perma.cc/9YAS-58VK*)

6 Europe v. Facebook, Get your Data!
http://www.europe-v-facebook.org/EN/Get_your_Data_/get_your_data_.html
(permanent copy *https://perma.cc/ABY9-N5RA*)

log in to the *social network* as well as numerous personal email addresses that the user never shared with Facebook and were most likely pulled from the contact list of his friends. It becomes apparent how easy it is to collect, save, and catalog data in the digital age; unfortunately, it is not as easy to request their deletion and, more importantly, to be certain of their destruction.

Schrems, after blacking out his personal information, decides to publish online the type of personal information contained in the report[7] attracting the attention of media, lawyers, politicians and regulators. When the movement reaches the Reddit platform community[8] , a large number of users send Facebook a request for access to their personal information in a similar way as Schrems did.

In August and September 2011, Schrems reported more than twenty[9] unlawful conduct by Facebook Ireland Ltd. to the Irish *Data Protection Commissioner.* Among the allegations made by Schrems is the lack of completeness of the personal information returned to him by the *social network*: Facebook refuses to provide certain categories of information, such as those related to biometric markers, claiming that it is a trade secret, and while it is understandable that the technology applied could be defined as proprietary, the reasoning given suggests that users' personal data are considered intellectual property of the company[10] .

The Irish commissioner's first report of nearly 150 pages[11] in response to the complaints filed by Schrems contains a number of recommendations with related considerations by the *social network* and a forecast for their implementation. The report and proposed suggestions are considered by the movement to be inadequate[12] to ensure the minimum requirements of European data protection law.

---

7 Europe v. Facebook, Facebook's Data Pool,
http://www.europe-v-facebook.org/EN/Data_Pool/data_pool.html
(permanent copy https://perma.cc/X9BL-VPZ4)

8 Reddit, How to annoy Facebook,
https://www.reddit.com/r/funny/comments/ktc16/how_to_annoy_facebook/
(permanent copy *https://perma.cc/R7VQ-73R4*)

9 Europe v. Facebook, Legal Procedure against "Facebook Ireland Limited."
http://www.europe-v-facebook.org/EN/Complaints/complaints.html
(permanent copy https://perma.cc/EL7H-E63S)

10 Forbes, Max Schrems: The Austrian Thorn In Facebook's Side,
https://www.forbes.com/sites/kashmirhill/2012/02/07/the-austrian-thorn-in-facebooks-side/
(permanent copy *https://perma.cc/Y7NW-5RW3*)

11 Europe v. Facebook, Facebook Ireland Ltd, Report of Audit,
http://www.europe-v-facebook.org/Facebook_Ireland_Audit_Report_Final.pdf
(permanent copy *https://perma.cc/4JQM-D6B2*)

12 Europe v. Facebook, Recent report on "Facebook Ireland Ltd."
http://www.europe-v-facebook.org/ODPC_JAN_pub.pdf

The battle against the *social network* ended in July 2014 when, almost three years after the filing of the twenty-two complaints, Schrems decided to withdraw the challenges, justifying the choice by the lack of a formal decision by the Irish commissioner guilty, in the opinion of the Europe v. Facebook movement, of failing to guarantee the most basic procedural rights (access to documents, evidence and counterclaims), cutting off all forms of communication and ignoring the reports made.

This event closes the first season of legal action by Schrems against Facebook and represents the beginning of the path that will lead to the first Schrems ruling. In fact, the movement decides to focus its efforts, including economic ones, on the appeal concerning the twenty-third complaint[13] , filed in June 2013 following Edward Joseph Snowden's revelations[14] and rejected by the Irish commissioner in October of that year, concerning the *PRISM* mass surveillance program.

NOYB

NOYB - European Center for Digital Rights, known more simply as *NOYB*[15] , *none of your business*, is a Vienna-based non-profit organization founded by Max Schrems in 2017. The organization's manifesto is summarized by the video posted on the YouTube platform[16] and re-released from the *NOYB* website page[17] in November 2017: "*Europe has the strictest privacy laws in the world and the right to privacy is also a fundamental right under European law but in practice the situation is different. [...] We want to make privacy a reality for everyone in Europe by collectively enforcing your right to privacy. [...] In 2018 a new European privacy law will come into force that has much better enforcement mechanisms. Since individual users will never*

(permanent copy https://perma.cc/5U59-AQDS)

13 Europe v. Facebook, Complaint against Facebook Ireland Ltd - 23 "PRISM", http://www.europe-v-facebook.org/prism/facebook.pdf (permanent copy https://perma.cc/48YQ-EFZT)

14 TED, Edward Snowden, https://www.ted.com/speakers/edward_snowden (permanent copy https://perma.cc/VKU9-MDB8)

15 NOYB, https://noyb.eu/en (permanent copy https://perma.cc/92E4-25T5)

16 YouTube, noyb.eu - #InvestInPrivacy [ENGLISH], https://www.youtube.com/watch?v=fKjHGaVkjJ4 (permanent copy https://perma.cc/QV6E-Q64C)

17 NOYB, Our Detailed Concept, https://noyb.eu/en/our-detailed-concept (permanent copy https://perma.cc/LKR9-ZHAS)

be able to go to court against big tech companies, the new law allows nonprofit organizations to defend your rights systematically and effectively! [...]"[18] .

NOYB's own page frames the organization's focus on commercial privacy and data protection violations because they are widespread, frequent, and affect millions of people. The organization also addresses all those companies that seek to comply with the law and are thus victims of unfair competition from companies pursuing illegal practices.

NOYB becomes operational on May 25, 2018, the date of implementation of the new General Data *Protection* Regulation, *General Data Protection Relation*, more commonly known by the acronym *GDPR. The* organization's activities are divided into three macro areas: legal actions, research projects, and awareness projects. The first area is the one of main interest in relation to the issues discussed in this paper: most of the complaints concern the transfer of personal data from Europe to the United States of America[19] and the repercussions resulting from the two Schrems rulings.

---

[18] Europe has the toughest privacy laws in the world.
Your right to privacy is even a fundamental right under European law!
But in practice, it sure does not feel like it ...
Corporations largely ignore your right to privacy - using your private information for their financial gain.
As a single user, you have to agree to absurd terms and put up with illegal misuse of your data -- unless you want to go offline and unfortunately this will only get worse as the digital transformation moves on.

We want to make privacy a reality for everybody in Europe, by collectively enforcing your right to privacy!
Over the last six years, we have successfully brought a number of model cases to make tech companies comply with the law.

In 2018 a new European privacy law will come into force that has much better enforcement mechanisms.
Because individual users will never be able to go to courts against big tech companies, the new law allows Non Profit Organizations to defend your rights!
We now want to use this law and set up a European Privacy Enforcement Organization that enforces your rights in a systematic and an effective way!
This is why we are asking for your help: If we find only 5,000 people worldwide to support us with 50 Euros per year, we would be ready to start within the next months ... if we find twice as many supporting members, we would be fully funded to fight for your rights!
We hope for your support for NOYB - for a digital future that respects your rights!

[19] NOYB, EU-US Data Transfers,
https://noyb.eu/en/project/eu-us-transfers
(permanent copy https://perma.cc/8YKN-4NZG)

Chapter 2.
The Schrems Judgment I

A proper assessment of the events surrounding the first Schrems ruling adopted by the Court of Justice of the European Union in October 2015 requires a preliminary analysis of the existing legislation in Europe related to the protection of personal data, the international agreements entered into between Europe and the United States of America on the overseas transfer of data of European citizens, and the particular historical context related to the revelations of Edward Joseph Snowden[20] about the *PRISM* mass surveillance program[21] of the U.S. government.

The complaint is submitted by Schrems[22] to the Irish *Data Protection Commissioner* in June 2013, a few days after Edward Joseph Snowden's first revelations, in a European regulatory environment that was still not adapted to the rapid technological change that had taken place in the preceding years. It is important to remember, and it will be detailed in the following pages, that in Europe in 2013 the processing of personal data is guaranteed by a number of EU measures, Directives 95/46/EC, 97/66/EC, 2002/58/EC as amended[23] , which have their roots in Convention 108[24] of the Council of Europe of 1981, also known as the Strasbourg Convention, and Article 8 of the European Convention on Human Rights[25] .

---

20 Wikipedia, Permanent Record (autobiography),
https://en.wikipedia.org/wiki/Permanent_Record_(autobiography)
(permanent copy https://perma.cc/G7BU-VBUW)

21 Wikipedia, PRISM (surveillance program),
https://en.wikipedia.org/wiki/PRISM_(surveillance_program)
(permanent copy *https://perma.cc/E7QX-QLR8*)

22 Europe v. Facebook, Complaint against Facebook Ireland Ltd - 23 "PRISM",
http://www.europe-v-facebook.org/prism/facebook.pdf
(permanent copy https://perma.cc/48YQ-EFZT)

23 Directive 2006/24/EC of the European Parliament and of the Council of March 15, 2006 on the retention of data generated or processed in connection with the provision of publicly available electronic communications services or of public communications networks and amending Directive 2002/58/EC
Directive 2009/136/EC of the European Parliament and of the Council of November 25, 2009 amending Directive 2002/22/EC on universal service and users' rights relating to electronic communications networks and services, Directive 2002/58/EC concerning the processing of personal data and the protection of privacy in the electronic communications sector and Regulation (EC) No. 2006/2004 on cooperation between national authorities responsible for the enforcement of consumer protection laws

24 Council of Europe Convention 108, Strasbourg Convention, Convention for the Protection of Individuals with regard to Automatic Processing of Personal Data,
https://rm.coe.int/1680078c45
(permanent copy https://perma.cc/28Z5-XX3J)

25 European Convention on Human Rights,
https://www.echr.coe.int/Documents/Convention_ITA.pdf
(permanent copy https://perma.cc/KXB9-QRAG)

While these guidelines have clearly identified the upheavals produced by the Internet in the traditional market structures for a wide range of electronic communication services, they are still inadequate in relation to the innovative technologies, typical of the world of *social networks* and more generally of the *net economy*[26] , for the mass collection and storage of personal information.

The regulatory environment

Directive 95/46/EC[27] of the Parliament and the Council of Europe of October 24, 1995, *on the protection of individuals with regard to the processing of personal data and on the free movement of such data*, entered into force on November 23, 1995, with its publication in the Official Journal of the European Communities L 281/31.

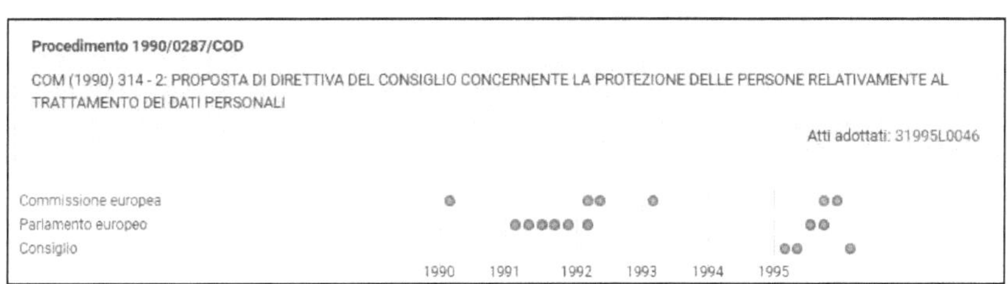

Figure 1 - Approval process of Directive 95/46/EC[28]

It consists of seventy-two recitals and thirty-three articles. Recitals 1 and 10, recalling the principles of the European Convention on Human Rights, clarify the purpose of the directive: to harmonize the rules on the protection of personal data in order to ensure their free movement among member states and to promote, at the same time, a high level of protection of citizens' fundamental rights. The need for harmonization arises from the fragmentation in this area among the different countries that are members of the European Community and a consequent need for approximation of national laws that would not, however, lead to a

---

[26] Wikipedia, New economy,
https://it.wikipedia.org/wiki/New_economy
(permanent copy https://perma.cc/B942-8VN6)

[27] Directive 95/46/EC of the European Parliament and of the Council of 24 October 1995 on the protection of individuals with regard to the processing of personal data and on the free movement of such data,
https://eur-lex.europa.eu/legal-content/IT/ALL/?uri=CELEX:31995L0046
(permanent copy https://perma.cc/MD4V-TPV5)

[28] Co-decision Procedure 1990/0287/COD on the proposal for a Council Directive on the protection of individuals with regard to the processing of personal data,
https://eur-lex.europa.eu/legal-content/IT/HIS/?uri=CELEX:31995L0046
(permanent copy https://perma.cc/GA8Q-E9R2)

weakening of the protection of individuals, and in this perspective, the directive leaves the acceding states very limited freedom of maneuver.

Article 2 provides the definitions relevant to the interpretation of the text, and it is interesting to note the foresight of the legislature, which, at the dawn of the *new economy*, manages to formulate definitions that will remain valid and applicable for more than two decades: personal data, "*any information concerning an identified or identifiable natural person [...] directly or indirectly, in particular by reference to an identification number or to one or more factors specific to his or her physical, physiological, mental, economic, cultural or social identity,*" personal data processing, "*any operation or set of operations which is performed upon personal data, whether or not by automated means, such as collection, recording, organization, storage, processing or alteration, retrieval, consultation, use, disclosure by transmission dissemination or any other form of making available, comparison or interconnection, as well as blocking, erasure or destruction,*" personal data file, "*any structured set of personal data that are accessible according to specified criteria, regardless of whether this set is centralized, decentralized or functionally or geographically distributed,*" and data subject's consent, "*any freely given, specific and informed indication of his or her wishes by which the data subject signifies his or her agreement to personal data relating to him or her being processed.*"

Article 12 guarantees any data subject the right to obtain from the controller "*freely and without constraint, [...] confirmation as to whether or not data relating to him or her are being processed, and information at least as to the purposes of the processing operations, the categories of data processed, the recipients or categories of recipients to whom the data are disclosed,*" and the possibility of requesting "the *rectification, erasure or blocking of data the processing of which does not comply with the provisions of the [...] Directive.*"

Article 25 regulates the transfer of personal data outside the European Economic Area[29] , prohibiting it if the destination state has a level of protection that does not meet European standards in a diametrically opposed approach to Convention 108, which considers any transfer to third countries to be lawful unless there are problems[30] . The directive thus aims to

---

29 Wikipedia, European Economic Area, https://en.wikipedia.org/wiki/European_Economic_Area (permanent copy https://perma.cc/7G3T-MDD4)

30 Council of Europe Convention 108, Strasbourg Convention for the Protection of Individuals with regard to Automatic Processing of Personal Data, Chapter III, Article 12 - International Flows of Personal Data and Domestic Law

create a safe zone in which to protect economic and productive activities from companies operating in countries that do not provide equal protections.

Article 26 provides exceptions to Article 25, i.e., in the case of a third country without an adequate level of protection, allowing a member state to authorize the transfer once it has received "*sufficient safeguards for the protection of the privacy and fundamental rights and freedoms of individuals and for the exercise of related rights*" from the controller and having informed the Commission and other member states.

Article 28 introduces independent supervisory authorities, the Supervisors, as an instrument for the proper implementation of the rules within the national territory. To this end, each supervisory authority has investigative powers[31] , effective powers of intervention[32] and the power to bring prosecutions in case of violation of national provisions implementing the directive.

The directive plays an instrumental role with respect to the need to break down borders within the European Community, allowing for the removal of limits on intangible transfers, but since it was adopted as a directive for the internal market, it has as its reference the regulation of trade, and both it and the national transposing laws conceive of data protection within a static relationship between the data owner and the data subject, in a proprietary view of the data itself favored by a formalistic enforcement through disclosures and consent. The fact that the data is the property of the data subject and cannot be used without consent means that for a long time the directive has been seen as a mere bureaucratic accomplishment to achieve the different goal of the Schengen Convention[33] . The Court of Justice of the European Union, based in Luxembourg, has jurisdiction over questions relating to the application of the directive and thus its interpretation. The application of the directive extends to the entire European Economic Area, thus far beyond the territory of the Union to include Iceland, Liechtenstein and Norway. The directive is implemented in Italy by Law 675/96[34] , *protection*

---

31 Right to access the data being processed and to collect any information necessary for the exercise of its supervisory function

32 To formulate opinions prior to the commencement of processing operations, in accordance with Article 20, and to give them adequate publicity, or that of ordering the freezing, erasure or destruction of data, or to temporarily or permanently prohibit a processing operation, or that of issuing a warning or warning to the controller, or that of referring the matter to national parliaments or other political institutions

33 Wikipedia, Schengen Convention,
https://it.wikipedia.org/wiki/Convenzione_di_Schengen
(permanent copy https://perma.cc/JQ7G-G87Z)

34 Law No. 675 of December 31, 1996, "Protection of persons and other subjects with regard to the processing of personal data," published in Official Gazette No. 5, January 8, 1997-Ordinary Supplement No. 3,
https://parlamento.it/parlam/leggi/96675l.htm
(permanent copy https://perma.cc/P8DR-PPBU)

of persons and other subjects with respect to the processing of personal data, also known as the Privacy Code, which will later be repealed by Legislative Decree 196/2003.

Directive 2002/58/EC[35] of the European Parliament and of the Council of July 12, 2002, *concerning the processing of personal data and the protection of privacy in the electronic communications sector (Directive on privacy and electronic communications)*, enters into force on July 31, 2002, with its publication in the Official Journal of the European Communities L 201/37. It consists of forty-nine recitals and twenty-one articles. More specifically, Article 3(1) specifies that the directive "shall *apply to the processing of personal data in connection with the provision of publicly available electronic communications services in public communications networks*" in the then European Community.

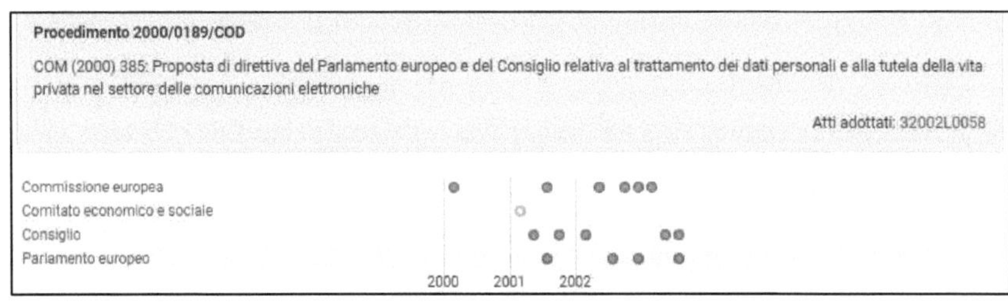

Figure 2 - Approval process of Directive 2002/58/EC[36]

Recitals 1 and 4, recall the protections provided by previous Directives 95/46/EC[37] , *on the protection of individuals with regard to the processing of personal data and on the free movement of such data*, and 97/66/EC[38] , *on the processing of personal data and the protection of privacy in the telecommunications sector*, and highlight the need to adapt

[35] Directive 2002/58/EC of the European Parliament and of the Council of 12 July 2002 concerning the processing of personal data and the protection of privacy in the electronic communications sector (Directive on privacy and electronic communications),
https://eur-lex.europa.eu/legal-content/IT/ALL/?uri=CELEX%3A32002L0058
(permanent copy https://perma.cc/43PE-BTSX)

[36] Codecision Procedure 2000/0189/COD on the Proposal for a Directive of the European Parliament and of the Council concerning the processing of personal data and the protection of privacy in the electronic communications sector,
https://eur-lex.europa.eu/legal-content/IT/HIS/?uri=CELEX:32002L0058
(permanent copy https://perma.cc/K5XZ-K2ZH)

[37] Directive 95/46/EC of the European Parliament and of the Council of 24 October 1995 on the protection of individuals with regard to the processing of personal data and on the free movement of such data,
https://eur-lex.europa.eu/legal-content/IT/TXT/?uri=CELEX:31995L0046
(permanent copy https://perma.cc/GK5E-JUEG)

[38] Directive 97/66/EC of the European Parliament and of the Council of December 15, 1997 concerning the processing of personal data and the protection of privacy in the telecommunications sector,
https://eur-lex.europa.eu/legal-content/IT/TXT/?uri=CELEX%3A31997L0066
(permanent copy https://perma.cc/U9CW-ARFS)

regulation "*to developments that have occurred in electronic communications services markets and technologies, so as to provide an equal level of protection of personal data and privacy to users of publicly available electronic communications services, regardless of the technologies used.*" Recital 2 highlights the need to respect the fundamental rights recognized in particular by the Charter of Fundamental Rights of the European Union[39] , also known as the Nice Charter. In particular, the directive aims to ensure full respect for the rights set forth in Articles 7[40] and 8[41] . Recitals 20 to 35 provide guidance for operators to take technical measures to ensure user privacy. In particular, recital 25 on so-called markers, also known as *cookies*, reports that "*they can be a legitimate and useful tool, for example for analyzing the effectiveness of website design and advertising, as well as for verifying the identity of transacting users,*" provided that clear, precise and understandable information on their operation is provided to the users themselves and that they can refuse their installation on their terminal.

The body of the directive begins by defining the purpose and scope, recalling in large part the statements made in the recitals, more specifically, Article 1(1) specifies that "*this Directive harmonizes the provisions of the Member States required to ensure an equivalent level of protection of fundamental rights and freedoms, and in particular the right to privacy, with respect to the processing of personal data in the electronic communications sector and to ensure the free movement of such data and of electronic communications equipment and services within the Community.*" It continues in the second article with definitions relevant to the interpretation of the text, in particular, it is interesting to note the definitions of user, "*any natural person using a publicly available electronic communications service, for private or business purposes, without necessarily being subscribed to it,*" communication, "*any information exchanged or transmitted between a finite number of parties by means of a publicly available electronic communications service,*" and user or subscriber consent, "*corresponds to the data subject's consent as referred to in Directive 95/46/EC*[42] ". Article 17

[39] Charter of Fundamental Rights of the European Union, Nice Charter, https://www.europarl.europa.eu/charter/pdf/text_it.pdf (permanent copy https://perma.cc/E4QG-VVMB)

[40] Article 7 of the Charter of Fundamental Rights of the European Union recognizes the right of everyone to enjoy respect for his or her private and family life, home and communications

[41] Article 8 of the Charter of Fundamental Rights of the European Union affirms the right of every individual to the protection of his or her personal data and the obligation of those who process such data to process them in accordance with the principle of fairness, for specified purposes and on the basis of the consent of the data subject or by reason of a legitimate interest provided by law. The article also affirms the data subject's right to access his or her data and to request its rectification

[42] Directive 95/46/EC of the European Parliament and of the Council of 24 October 1995 on the protection of individuals with regard to the processing of personal data and on the free movement of such data, Chapter I -

defines the obligation for member states to implement the directive by October 31, 2003, while Article 19 provides for the repeal of Directive 97/66/EC as of the same date. Also noteworthy is Article 18, which introduces an automatic review mechanism for the directive, requiring the Commission to submit a report every three years on its implementation and its impact on economic operators and consumers in relation to the international context.

The requirements are implemented in our system by Legislative Decree 196/2003[43] , *a code on the protection of personal data*, which with its one hundred and eighty-six articles also brings order to the matter after two laws, nine legislative decrees and two decrees of the President of the Republic had been issued since 1996.

Directive 2002/58/EC is being amended, as also provided in Article 18, by the two Directives 2006/24/EC[44] and 2009/136/EC[45] .

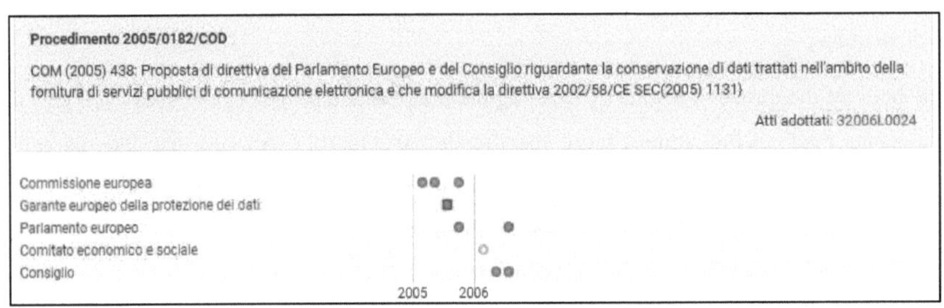

Figure 3 - Approval process of Directive 2006/24/EC[46]

General Provisions, Article 2 - Definitions, paragraph h, "consent of the data subject" means any freely given specific and informed indication of his or her wishes by which the data subject signifies his or her agreement to personal data relating to him or her being processed

43 Legislative Decree No. 196 of June 30, 2003, "Code for the Protection of Personal Data," published in Official Gazette No. 174 of July 29, 2003-Ordinary Supplement No. 123, *https://web.camera.it/parlam/leggi/deleghe/testi/03196dl.htm* (permanent copy https://perma.cc/74UQ-VGGG)

44 Directive 2006/24/EC of the European Parliament and of the Council of March 15, 2006 on the retention of data generated or processed in connection with the provision of publicly available electronic communications services or of public communications networks and amending Directive 2002/58/EC, *https://eur-lex.europa.eu/legal-content/IT/TXT/?uri=celex:32006L0024* (permanent copy https://perma.cc/HWK6-FYKT)

45 Directive 2009/136/EC of the European Parliament and of the Council of November 25, 2009, amending Directive 2002/22/EC on universal service and users' rights relating to electronic communications networks and services, Directive 2002/58/EC concerning the processing of personal data and the protection of privacy in the electronic communications sector and Regulation (EC) No. 2006/2004 on cooperation between national authorities responsible for the enforcement of consumer protection laws, *https://eur-lex.europa.eu/legal-content/IT/TXT/?uri=CELEX%3A32009L0136* (permanent copy https://perma.cc/NQY6-6H5C)

46 Codecision Procedure 2005/0182/COD on the Proposal for a Directive of the European Parliament and of the Council on the retention of data processed in connection with the provision of public electronic communication services and amending Directive 2002/58/EC,

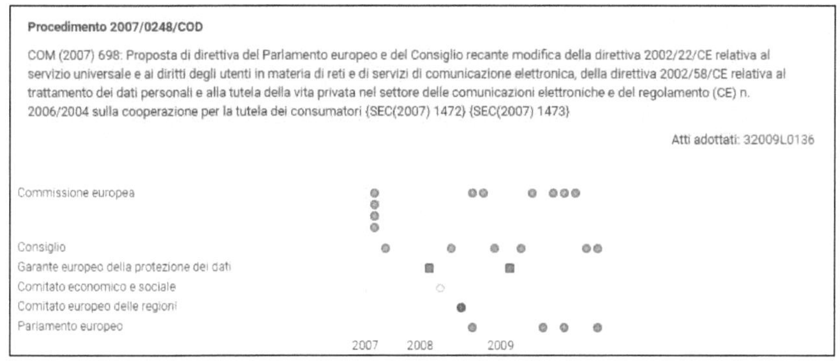

Figure 4 - Approval process of Directive 2009/136/EC[47]

Of particular interest are the changes introduced in particular by the Second Directive with the simplification of Article 3, "*The Directive shall apply to the processing of personal data in connection with the provision of publicly available electronic communications services in public communications networks in the Community, including public communications networks supporting data collection and identification devices.*" the renaming of Article 4 from "*Security*" to "*Security of Processing,*" with the adoption of minimum measures to ensure it, and the insertion of the adverb "*preliminarily*" in the third paragraph of Article 6, to indicate the need for acquisition of consent for the lawfulness of processing. The requirements of the directive are implemented, in our system, with the promulgation of Legislative Decree 69/2012[48] , *amendments to Legislative Decree No. 196 of June 30, 2003, bearing code on the protection of personal data in implementation of Directives 2009/136/EC, on the processing of personal data and the protection of privacy in the electronic communications sector [...].*

---

https://eur-lex.europa.eu/legal-content/IT/HIS/?uri=CELEX:32006L0024
(permanent copy https://perma.cc/X6RH-NHA3)

[47] Co-decision Procedure 2007/0248/COD on the Proposal for a Directive of the European Parliament and of the Council amending Directive 2002/22/EC on universal service and users' rights relating to electronic communications networks and services, Directive 2002/58/EC concerning the processing of personal data and the protection of privacy in the electronic communications sector and Regulation (EC) No. 2006/2004 on consumer protection cooperation,
https://eur-lex.europa.eu/legal-content/IT/HIS/?uri=CELEX:32009L0136
(permanent copy https://perma.cc/33BH-7PMG)

[48] Legislative Decree No. 69 of May 28, 2012, "Amendments to Legislative Decree No. 196 of June 30, 2003, setting forth the Personal Data Protection Code in implementation of Directives 2009/136/EC on the processing of personal data and the protection of privacy in the electronic communications sector and 2009/140/EC on electronic communications networks and services and Regulation (EC) No. 2006/2004 on cooperation between national authorities responsible for the enforcement of consumer protection laws," published in Official Gazette No. 126 of May 31, 2012,
https://www.gazzettaufficiale.it/eli/id/2012/05/31/012G0090/sg
(permanent copy https://perma.cc/26K4-PD7L)

The Safe Harbor

The Anglo-Saxon expression safe harbor[49], in Italian safe harbor, indicates in jurisprudence a rule or principle that certain conduct is not regarded as a violation of a more general rule. Similarly, the expression *unsafe harbor* indicates conduct that is certainly designated as a violation.

The *safe harbor* concept makes it possible to reduce the uncertainty created by a general but imprecise rule by allowing legislators to prescribe with certainty the anticipated outcome for specific foreseeable cases, and to leave the decision on the remaining cases to the courts.

On July 26, 2000, the European Commission adopted Decision 2000/520/EC[50] concluding an agreement between the then European Community and the United States of America for the free overseas transfer, for commercial purposes, of European citizens' data by European multinational companies. The decision refers to the *Safe Harbor Privacy Principles*[51] published by the U.S. Department of Commerce on July 21, 2000, in particular Article 1 specifies that "*for the purposes of applying Article 25(2) of Directive 95/46/EC, [...] the Safe Harbor Privacy Principles [...] shall be deemed to ensure an adequate level of protection for personal data transferred from the Community to organizations established in the United States.*" U.S. companies operating in the European Economic Area must comply with and certify compliance with seven principles set forth in the *Safe Harbor Privacy Principles*: notification[52], choice[53], transfer[54], security[55], integrity[56], access[57], adequacy[58].

---

49 Wikipedia, Safe harbor (law), https://en.wikipedia.org/wiki/Safe_harbor_(law) (permanent copy https://perma.cc/9CPP-7XCG)

50 Commission Decision 2000/520/EC of July 26, 2000, pursuant to Directive 95/46/EC of the European Parliament and of the Council on the adequacy of the protection afforded by the Safe Harbor Principles and related "Frequently Asked Questions" (FAQs) on privacy published by the U.S. Department of Commerce, https://eur-lex.europa.eu/legal-content/IT/TXT/?uri=CELEX%3A32000D0520 (permanent copy https://perma.cc/UX7L-XACB)

51 Export.gov, Safe Harbor Privacy Principles, issued by the U.S. Department of Commerce on July 21, 2000, https://2016.export.gov/safeharbor/eu/eg_main_018475.asp (permanent copy https://perma.cc/BGD2-XU55)

52 Organizations must inform individuals about the purposes for which information is collected and used in clear language

53 Organizations must offer individuals a choice (faculty of refusal) as to whether personal information should be disclosed to third parties, or used for purposes incompatible with those for which it was originally collected

54 Organizations disclosing information to third parties must apply the principles of notice and choice by ensuring a level of confidentiality protection appropriate to European law

55 Organizations that hold, update, use, or disseminate personal information must take reasonable precautions to protect it from loss and misuse as well as from unauthorized access, disclosure, alteration, and destruction

56 Personal information must be relevant to the purposes for which it was collected or those subsequently authorized by the data subjects by ensuring that the data are reliable, accurate, complete, and up-to-date

The decision is implemented, in our system, by Resolution No. 36[59] of October 10, 2001, in which the Privacy Guarantor authorizes "*transfers of personal data from the territory of the State to organizations based in the United States made on the basis of and in accordance with the 'Safe Harbor Principles on Confidentiality'.*"

In the following years, numerous European Commission reports could verify and testify to the lack of transparency and non-compliance by U.S. companies[60] *with the Safe Harbor Privacy Principles.*

The complaint

The complaint that led to the adoption of the measure of the Court of Justice of the European Union known as the Schrems I ruling originated in the summer of 2013 with the revelations of Edward Joseph Snowden[61] . Snowden's story, well told in the film of the same name[62] , can be briefly summarized in the events below. On May 20, 2013, Snowden, a former *CIA* technician, left his job at a consultant information technology firm at an *NSA* facility[63] , the U.S. National Security Agency, in Hawaii and flew to Hong Kong. The trip has been planned for months: he has been closing his bank accounts, wiping and encrypting his old computers

---

57 Individuals should have access to personal information about themselves held by a given organization, and also be able to correct, amend, or delete it

58 In order to effectively protect the privacy of personal data, mechanisms must be in place to ensure compliance with the principles, recourse for individuals to whom the data relate who see their interests harmed by non-compliance with the principles, and non-punity for an organization that fails to comply with the principles including through sanctions that are sufficiently stringent to ensure that organizations comply with the principles

59 Data Protection Authority, Authorization for transfer to the United States of America ('Safe Harbor') - October 10, 2001,
https://www.garanteprivacy.it/home/docweb/-/docweb-display/docweb/30939
(permanent copy https://perma.cc/NJX9-RVV6)

60 Commission Staff Working Paper, The application of Commission Decision 520/2000/EC of 26 July 2000 pursuant to Directive 95/46 of the European Parliament and of the Council on the adequate protection of personal data provided by the Safe Harbour Privacy Principles and related Frequently Asked Questions issued by the US Department of Commerce,
*https://ec.europa.eu/transparency/documents-register/api/files/SEC(2002)196_0/de00000863263?*rendition=false
(permanent copy *https://perma.cc/WUF4-B47R*)

61 Wikipedia, Permanent Record (autobiography),
https://en.wikipedia.org/wiki/Permanent_Record_(autobiography)
(permanent copy https://perma.cc/G7BU-VBUW)

62 MyMovies.co.uk, Snowden,
https://www.mymovies.it/film/2016/snowden/
(permanent copy https://perma.cc/5G5R-TCG6)

63 NSA/CSS, National Security Agency/Central Security Service,
https://www.nsa.gov/
(permanent copy https://perma.cc/2RNX-TMUA)

to erase all traces, taking with him four laptops[64] and conducting all cash transactions. In early June, at The Mira Hong Kong Hotel[65] where he is staying, he secretly meets with Laura Poitras[66] (U.S. film director, film producer and documentary filmmaker), Glenn Greenwald[67] and Ewen MacAskill (journalists from The Guardian newspaper) to whom he reveals the existence of several U.S. government mass surveillance programs. The revelations are supported by numerous documents leaked during his time at the *NSA* and highlight an intrusive level of surveillance, which through access to data managed by large *hi-tech* companies, such as Apple, Facebook, Google, Microsoft and Yahoo, appears to be not limited to U.S. territory but extended to the rest of the world. On June 6, 2013, The British newspaper The Guardian publishes the first revelations about the *PRISM* program[68] , a few days later Snowden's identity is revealed by the publication of Laura Poitras' video interview[69] on The Guardian website. On June 14, 2013, Snowden is formally charged with espionage by the U.S. government and an extradition request is issued against him. He manages to reach Moscow where, on August 1, 2013, after making requests for political asylum to twenty-seven countries, the Russian government grants him temporary asylum.

In light of these revelations, on June 25, 2013, Schrems submits his twenty-third complaint[70] to Ireland's *Data Protection Commissioner* against Facebook Ireland Ltd. believed to be guilty of violating the Irish *Data Protection Act* and Directive 95/46/EC to which it refers.

The complaint refers to the twenty-two previous complaints, which have yet to be adjudicated, and draws the commissioner's attention to the fact that the service offered by Facebook outside the territory of the United States of America and Canada is provided by

---

64 One computer is intended for secure communications, one for traditional communications, one to be used as a decoy, and a fourth device that has never been, and never will be, connected to any network

65 The Mira Hong Kong Hotel, *https://www.themirahotel.com/hong-kong/en/* (permanent copy https://perma.cc/MY85-6EVH)

66 Wikipedia, Laura Poitras, *https://it.wikipedia.org/wiki/Laura_Poitras* (permanent copy https://perma.cc/LG5F-J3WL)

67 Wikipedia, Glenn Greenwald, *https://it.wikipedia.org/wiki/Glenn_Greenwald* (permanent copy https://perma.cc/K4TB-6QBX)

68 The Guardian, NSA Prism program taps in to user data of Apple, Google and others, *https://www.theguardian.com/world/2013/jun/06/us-tech-giants-nsa-data* (permanent copy *https://perma.cc/KV8J-7G9D*)

69 The Guardian, Edward Snowden: the whistleblower behind the NSA surveillance revelations, *https://www.theguardian.com/world/2013/jun/09/edward-snowden-nsa-whistleblower-surveillance* (permanent copy *https://perma.cc/H2RZ-4TR3*)

70 Europe v. Facebook, Complaint against Facebook Ireland Ltd - 23 "PRISM", *http://www.europe-v-facebook.org/prism/facebook.pdf* (permanent copy https://perma.cc/48YQ-EFZT)

Facebook Ireland Ltd. which, however, makes a transfer to Facebook Inc. for the actual management and processing of the data.

In Schrems' opinion, this transfer is not necessary: personal data of European citizens could be stored on European territory, or in the European Economic Area, and their transfer is likely to be dictated by economic reasons.

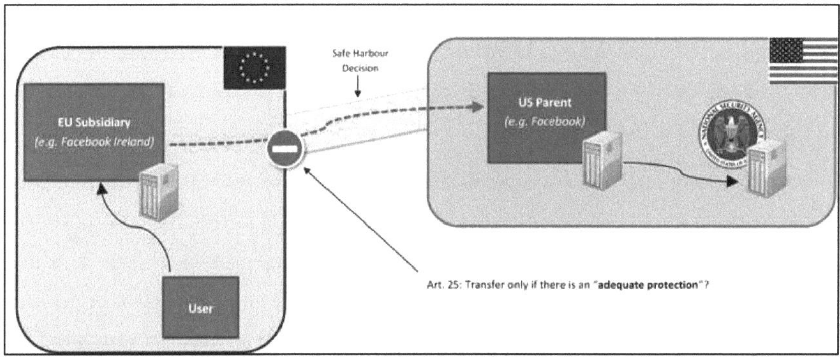

Figure 5 - Safe Harbor EU-US[71]

Snowden's revelations published by the British newspaper The Guardian show that Facebook Inc. allows massive access to the personal data of platform users by the *NSA* for reasons of espionage and national security, without the need for just cause, under a program called *PRISM*. Published documents show that Facebook Inc.'s adherence to the *PRISM* program is voluntary and that new services have been developed over time demonstrating close cooperation with the government agency. Schrems points out that there is no obvious reason to doubt these revelations: the first comments by President Barack Obama[72] and Director of National Intelligence James Clapper[73] after the publication of The Guardian article did not deny government access to the *servers* of Facebook Inc. and the other companies involved in the scandal; if the newspaper's allegations were unfounded, it would have been logical to reject them clearly and unequivocally. At the same time, the companies involved are,

[71] Europe v. Facebook, "PRISM" Complaints against Facebook, Apple, Skype, Microsoft and Yahoo! *http://www.europe-v-facebook.org/EN/Complaints/Safe_Harbor/safe_harbor.html* (permanent copy *https://perma.cc/F738-Z3GM*)

[72] The New York Times, Obama Calls Surveillance Programs Legal and Limited, *https://www.nytimes.com/2013/06/08/us/national-security-agency-surveillance.html* (permanent copy *https://perma.cc/5XRF-TCBW*)

[73] U.S. News & World Report, Spy Chief Says Taps Analyzed Only for 'Reasonable Suspicion', *https://www.usnews.com/news/articles/2013/06/07/spy-chief-says-taps-analyzed-only-for-reasonable-suspicion* (permanent copy *https://perma.cc/D4VM-7MW9*)

according to their own statements, subject to secrecy so Facebook Inc.'s statements cannot prove or disprove their cooperation with the *NSA*.

The complaint filed by Schrems can thus be summarized in three key points: Facebook Ireland Ltd. is the controller of the data and has outsourced its management to Facebook Inc.; Facebook Inc. is likely to allow access to the *servers by* the *NSA* even without just cause; and Facebook Inc.'s claims are unreliable by virtue of a secrecy bond with the U.S. government. Based on these considerations, Schrems asks the Irish commissioner to clarify the facts by placing the burden of proof on Facebook Ireland Ltd. as to the falsity or inaccuracy of the facts revealed by The Guardian.

Schrems' argument states that data acquired by Facebook Ireland Ltd. are transferred to Facebook Inc. in the absence of an adequate level of protection as required by Article 25 of Directive 95/46/EC and consequently the Irish *Data Protection Act.* A transfer to a third country without an adequate level of protection is permissible under Article 26 of the same directive if "*the data subject has unambiguously consented to the* intended *transfer*"[74] and "*where the data controller provides sufficient safeguards for the protection of the privacy and fundamental rights and freedoms of individuals and for the exercise of* related *rights.*"[75] . This possibility is not applicable to the case under consideration by virtue of the fact that Facebook Ireland Ltd. and Facebook Inc. deny any kind of cooperation with the *NSA* therefore the transfer must necessarily be subject to the *safe harbor* regime. Schrems thus highlights the failure to comply with the *Safe Harbor Privacy* Principles, particularly the Notice and Choice Principles, due to the massive transfer in favor of the government agency.

Four similar complaints are filed with the Irish commissioner for multinational Apple[76] , the Luxembourg commission, *Nationale Kommission für den Datenschutz,* for Microsoft[77] and

---

[74] Directive 95/46/EC of the European Parliament and of the Council of 24 October 1995 on the protection of individuals with regard to the processing of personal data and on the free movement of such data, Chapter IV - Transfer of personal data to third countries, Article 26 - Exemptions, paragraph 1, subparagraph a)

[75] Directive 95/46/EC of the European Parliament and of the Council of 24 October 1995 on the protection of individuals with regard to the processing of personal data and on the free movement of such data, Chapter IV - Transfer of personal data to third countries, Article 26 - Exceptions, paragraph 2

[76] Europe v. Facebook, Complaint against "Apple Distribution International," a complaint filed in Ireland regarding the transfer operated by "Apple Distribution International" (Ireland) to "Apple Inc." (USA), http://www.europe-v-facebook.org/prism/apple.pdf
(permanent copy https://perma.cc/A98S-6YYV)

[77] Europe v. Facebook, Antrag auf Einhaltung meiner Grundrechte (Art 32 Abs 4 DSG), complaint filed in Luxembourg regarding the transfer operated by "Microsoft Luxembourg" to "Microsoft Corporation" (USA), http://www.europe-v-facebook.org/prism/microsoft.pdf
(permanent copy https://perma.cc/LKR9-N8R5)

Skype[78] , and the Bavarian office, *Bayerisches Landesamt für Datenschutzaufsicht*, for Yahoo![79] .

The Irish commissioner, as anticipated earlier, rejects the complaint and will never initiate an investigation, calling the allegation "frivolous and vexatious."[80] . The Luxembourg commission states that the *safe harbor* transfer of data would be illegal if the data were transmitted to the *NSA* however states that it cannot confirm the existence of the *PRISM* program[81] . Access to documents and evidence related to the proceedings will never be allowed and no judgment will ever be issued. The Bavarian office forwards the complaint to the German federal authority, *Bundesbeauftragter für den Datenschutz und die Informationsfreiheit*, which will confirm that it has initiated proceedings[82] that will never lead to the issuance of a judgment.

Schrems, still a doctoral student in law at the University of Vienna, then decided to focus his efforts, including economic ones, on a single complaint, the one related to the transfer made by Facebook Ireland Ltd. to Facebook Inc. and on Oct. 23, 2013, he filed an application for review[83] in the Irish *High Court* against the inaction shown by the Irish commissioner. The application for review is granted by the Irish High Court[84] . On June 18, 2014, Judge Gerard

---

78 Europe v. Facebook, Antrag auf Einhaltung meiner Grundrechte (Art 32 Abs 4 DSG), complaint filed in Luxembourg regarding the transfer operated by "Skype Technologies S.à.r.l." to "Microsoft Corporation" (USA),
http://www.europe-v-facebook.org/prism/skype.pdf
(permanent copy https://perma.cc/NY89-KAF4)

79 Europe v. Facebook, Beschwerde gegen die "Yahoo! Deutschland GmbH," complaint filed in Germany regarding the transfer operated by "Yahoo! Deutschland GmbH" to "Yahoo! Inc." (USA),
http://www.europe-v-facebook.org/prism/yahoo.pdf
(permanent copy https://perma.cc/8SMS-SWDA)

80 Raidió Teilifís Éireann, Ireland's National Public Service Media, Data Protection Commissioner says no action will be taken against Apple and Facebook,
https://www.rte.ie/news/2013/0726/464770-data-protection/
(permanent copy https://perma.cc/5EYG-V4S8)

81 National Commission for Data Protection, Grand-Duchy of Luxembourg, Presentation of the annual report,
https://cnpd.public.lu/en/actualites/national/2014/05/rapport-annuel-2013.html
(permanent copy *https://perma.cc/PAL6-XMA9*)

82 Bundesbeauftragter für den Datenschutz und die Informationsfreiheit, Entschließung der Konferenz der Datenschutzbeauftragten des Bundes und der Länder vom 5. September 2013,
*https://www.bfdi.bund.de/SharedDocs/Downloads/DE/DSK/DSKEntschliessungen/DSK_20130905_EntschliessungUeberwNachrichtend.*html
(permanent copy *https://perma.cc/TX92-YCR5*)

83 Europe v. Facebook, The High Court Judicial Review, Record No. 2013/765/JR,
http://www.europe-v-facebook.org/JR_Grounding_Documents.pdf
(permanent copy https://perma.cc/A6VG-XB5J)

84 The Telegraph, Facebook 'PRISM' decision to be reviewed by Irish High Court,
https://www.telegraph.co.uk/technology/facebook/10401419/Facebook-PRISM-decision-to-be-reviewed-by-Irish-High-Court.html
(permanent copy *https://perma.cc/7N32-ZM85*)

Hogan[85] adjourns the case[86] stating that the Irish legislation is subject to European law, more specifically Directive 95/46/EC and Decision 2000/520/EC on the *safe harbor* regime, so he decides to refer the decision back to the Court of Justice of the European Union[87] as the central issue is a re-evaluation of the two pieces of legislation in relation to Article 8 of the Charter of Fundamental Rights of the European Union[88] .

The judgment

The procedure before the Court of Justice of the European Union is C-362/14[89] . The hearing before the Court of Justice of the European Union is held on March 24, 2015. The attorney general of the court is Yves Bot[90] . During the hearing the counsel for the European Commission admits that Decision 2000/520/EC failed to ensure an adequate level for data protection[91] . On this occasion, part of the documents produced at the beginning of the proceedings become public knowledge, in particular, the report filed in November 2014 by Dr. Franziska Bohm[92] regarding the adequacy of *Safe Harbor*[93] . The document highlights the profound differences between the guarantees provided by Directive 95/46/EC and those

---

85 Wikipedia, Gerard Hogan,
https://en.wikipedia.org/wiki/Gerard_Hogan
(permanent copy https://perma.cc/AQX3-MFD7)

86 Europe v. Facebook, The High Court Judgment of Mr. Justice Hogan delivered on the 18th June, 2014,
http://www.europe-v-facebook.org/hcj.pdf
(permanent copy https://perma.cc/MJF2-CRRV)

87 Treaty on the Functioning of the European Union, Article 267, Reference for a preliminary ruling.

88 Everyone has the right to the protection of personal data concerning him or her. Such data must be processed in accordance with the principle of fairness, for specified purposes, and on the basis of the data subject's consent or other legitimate basis provided by law. Every individual has the right to access and obtain rectification of the data collected concerning him or her. Compliance with these rules is subject to monitoring by an independent authority

89 Court of Justice of the European Union, case number C-362/14,
https://curia.europa.eu/juris/documents.jsf?oqp=&for=&mat=or&lgrec=de&jge=&td=%3BALL&jur=C%2CT%2CF&num=C-362%252F14&page=1&dates=&pcs=Oor&lg=&pro=&nat=or&cit=none%252
CC%252CCJ%252CR%252C2008E%252C%252C%252C%252C%252C%252C%252C%252C%252C%252C%252Ctrue%252Cfalse%252Cfalse&language=en&avg=&cid=19827
(permanent copy https://perma.cc/6G7J-FLRG)

90 Wikipedia, Yves Bot,
https://en.wikipedia.org/wiki/Yves_Bot
(permanent copy https://perma.cc/CJM8-KBZ9)

91 EUobserver, EU-US data pact skewered in court hearing,
https://euobserver.com/justice/128131
(permanent copy https://perma.cc/N4AW-HJPH)

92 FIZ Karlsruhe - Leibniz Institute for Information Infrastructure, Prof. Dr. Franziska Boehm,
https://www.fiz-karlsruhe.de/de/forschung/publikationen-prof-dr-franziska-boehm
(permanent copy https://perma.cc/RB9J-VAWZ)

93 Prof. Dr. Franziska Boehm, Opinion on the adequacy of the Safe Harbor Decision, Comparison between Safe Harbor and Directive 95/46, Case 362/14,
https://www.zar.kit.edu/DATA/veroeffentlichungen/237_Legal_opinion_SH_Boehm_100603a.pdf
(permanent copy *https://perma.cc/D7F5-6ZWF*)

actually offered by the EU-US agreement: the mechanism of self-certification of companies and the absence of active and independent control over the proper processing of data are contrary to what is provided for in European legislation.

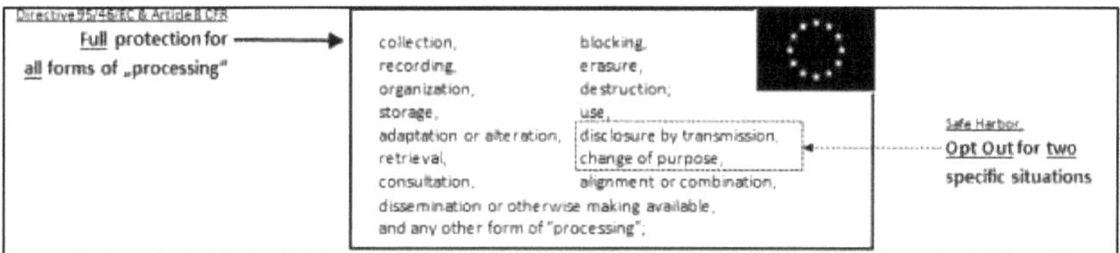

Figure 6 - Safe Harbor Adequacy Assessment[94]

The Advocate General delivers his opinion[95] on September 23, 2015 stating the need for a reassessment of the decision following the events that have occurred in the meantime and taking into account the current factual and legal context. The opinion concludes with *the* paragraph "*Commission Decision 2000/520/EC of July 26, 2000 [...] is invalid.*"

The court issues its ruling on October 6, 2015, declaring that "*Decision 2000/520 is invalid.*": the *safe harbor* regime does not provide guarantees regarding U.S. government interference, does not guarantee individuals the right of access to correct, amend or delete data, and does not allow for oversight by the independent supervisory authorities of European countries. On November 30, 2015, the judgment, which will remain known as the "Schrems I Judgment," is published in the Official Journal of the European Union C 398/5[96] .

The ruling, recalling Article 25, which prohibits the transfer of personal data outside the European Economic Area in the absence of a level of protection that does not meet European

---

[94] Prof. Dr. Franziska Boehm, Opinion on the adequacy of the Safe Harbor Decision, Comparison between Safe Harbor and Directive 95/46, Case 362/14, page 13, *https://www.zar.kit.edu/DATA/veroeffentlichungen/237_Legal_opinion_SH_Boehm_100603a.pdf* (permanent copy *https://perma.cc/D7F5-6ZWF*)

[95] Court of Justice of the European Union, Opinion of Advocate General Yves Bot delivered on September 23, 2015, Case C-362/14, *https://curia.europa.eu/juris/document/document.jsf?text=&docid=168421&pageIndex=0&doclang=IT&* mode=lst&dir=&occ=first&part=1&cid=253155 (permanent copy https://perma.cc/W2GC-URMS)

[96] Judgment of the Court (Grand Chamber) of October 6, 2015, Case C-362/14 - reference for a preliminary ruling from the High Court (Ireland) - Maximilian Schrems v. Data Protection Commissioner, *https://eur-lex.europa.eu/legal-content/IT/TXT/?uri=CELEX%3A62014CA0362* (permanent copy https://perma.cc/977Z-93LP)

standards, thus affirms that the United States of America is to be regarded as a country with lower standards of personal data protection[97] .

The ruling is transposed, in our system, by Order No. 564[98] of October 22, 2015, by which the Personal Data Protection Authority orders "*the lapsing of the authorization adopted by the Garante on October 10, 2001 by resolution No. 36 and for the effect prohibits, in accordance with Articles 154, paragraph 1, lett. d) and 45 of the Code, the exporting entities from transferring, on the basis of that resolution and the prerequisites indicated therein, personal data from the territory of the State to the United States of America.*"

It is interesting to note that the *Swiss Federal Data Protection and Information Commissioner ("SDPIC")* will also invalidate the similar existing agreement between Switzerland and the United States of America, *U.S.-Swiss Safe Harbor*[99] , following the ruling of the Court of Justice of the European Union.

With the annulment of the *Safe Harbor*, EU-US data transfers cannot be made on the basis of self-certification but on the stipulation of "standard contractual clauses" that, by ensuring an adequate level of protection, authorize their processing[100] . In the absence of agreements, large U.S. *hi-tech* companies would be forced to stop transferring data overseas or build *data centers* in Europe in which to handle the data of European citizens.

On December 1, 2015, Schrems re-submits his complaint against Facebook to the Irish commissioner[101] and sends similar complaints to the Belgian commission[102] , *Commission for*

---

[97] Raidió Teilifís Éireann, Ireland's National Public Service Media, European court online data ruling welcomed,
https://www.rte.ie/news/2015/1006/732665-safe-harbour-ecj/
(permanent copy https://perma.cc/F9GZ-NXHQ)

[98] Garante per la Protezione dei Dati Personali, Transfer of personal data to the U.S.: Caducazione provvedimento del Garante del 10.10.2001 di riconoscimento dell'accordo sul c.d.c. "Safe Harbor" - October 22, 2015,
https://www.garanteprivacy.it/web/guest/home/docweb/-/docweb-display/docweb/4396484
(permanent copy https://perma.cc/VA68-B9FZ)

[99] Export.gov, U.S.-Swiss Safe Harbor Overview,
https://2016.export.gov/safeharbor/swiss/eg_main_018519.asp
(permanent copy https://perma.cc/2J4K-DDHK)

[100] The Guardian, What is 'safe harbor' and why did the EUCJ just declare it invalid?
https://www.theguardian.com/technology/2015/oct/06/safe-harbour-european-court-declare-invalid-data-protection
(permanent copy *https://perma.cc/WQ2A-XJKH*)

[101] Europe v. Facebook, Complaint against Facebook Ireland Ltd,
http://www.europe-v-facebook.org/comp_fb_ie.pdf
(permanent copy https://perma.cc/L84W-4QGE)

[102] Europe v. Facebook, Beschwerde gegen "Facebook Ireland Ltd", "Facebook Inc" und/oder die Facebook-Niederlassung in Brüssel,
http://www.europe-v-facebook.org/comp_fb_be.pdf
(permanent copy https://perma.cc/62EQ-9CES)

the Protection of Privacy, and the German commissioner[103] , *Hamburgische Beauftragte für Datenschutz und Informationsfreiheit*, which have jurisdiction over local subsidiaries. The complaints are aimed at enforcing the ruling of the Court of Justice of the European Union. The outcome of these complaints is not significant for evaluations related to the ECJ ruling; in the following years, the activism of Schrems and his supporters will confront *GDPR*, the new European data protection regulation, leading to the second Schrems ruling.

Evaluations

To elaborate on the significance of the ECJ's ruling, it is useful to refer to the reflections published by Schrems himself on the Europe v. Facebook movement website[104] regarding possible alternatives, in the absence of *safe harbor*, for allowing the overseas transfer of European citizens' personal data.

Schrems believes that many *B2C* companies, which includes large *hi-tech* companies, will simply add a paragraph in the *privacy policy* with a typically American legal approach that is bound to fail under European law: consent to U.S. mass surveillance will have to comply with the European Union's strict rules on consent to processing. The inclusion of a simple notice, such as "*the data is being transferred outside the European Economic Area*" or "*we may process your personal information on a server located outside the country where you live*," is not enough to make it clear to an average user, clearly and unambiguously, that his or her data could be processed by the *NSA*. Real informed consent should be much more direct and explain to users that the data collected may be subject to mass surveillance programs, indiscriminately, by the U.S. government in total contravention of the secrecy constraint to which corporations are subject. It is important then to remember that consent must be free, but no user will freely ask to provide his or her data to the *NSA* rather will accept the disclosure in order not to be excluded from the most common communication tools of the new generation.

Thus, Schrems argues that a large number of companies will move toward contractual solutions for *B2B* data transfers[105] through the establishment of model contract clauses[106] or

---

[103] Europe v. Facebook, Beschwerde gegen "Facebook Ireland Ltd", "Facebook Inc" und/oder die "Facebook Germany GmbH",
http://www.europe-v-facebook.org/comp_fb_de.pdf
(permanent copy https://perma.cc/YDJ4-R22E)

[104] Europe v. Facebook, First Thoughts on Decision C-362/14,
http://www.europe-v-facebook.org/EN/Complaints/Safe_Harbor/Response/response.html
(permanent copy https://perma.cc/D9Y7-JF3N)

[105] Directive 95/46/EC of the European Parliament and of the Council of 24 October 1995 on the protection of

binding corporate rules[107] : sets of contractual terms and conditions signed by the sender and recipient of personal data to ensure respect for the rights and freedoms of the individual. This solution is a viable alternative for companies not adhering to surveillance programs but is bound to fail, even from a legal standpoint, for others.

In the days immediately following the ruling of the Court of Justice of the European Union, Schrems is convinced that a "*Safe Harbor 2.0*" decision is not feasible any time soon: the European Commission and the U.S. government should start again with an analysis of the requirements. The self-certification mechanism proved unable to ensure adequate data processing: the term "*adequate*" was ambiguous, associated with a concept of "*basic protection*" rather than the concept of "*substantially equivalent*" as clarified by the ruling. Detection and oversight mechanisms were found to be ineffective, and the European country supervisors had no way to act to prohibit data transfers. In the absence of an overhaul of U.S. laws, the existence of a mass surveillance program will therefore result in a separation of products, for U.S. users and European users, to ensure the location of data and its proper processing.

individuals with regard to the processing of personal data and on the free movement of such data, Chapter IV - Transfer of personal data to third countries, Article 26 - Exceptions, paragraph 2

[106] SCC - Standard Contractual Clauses, Commission Decision 2010/87/EU of February 5, 2010 on standard contractual clauses for the transfer of personal data to processors established in third countries under Directive 95/46/EC of the European Parliament and of the Council, https://eur-lex.europa.eu/legal-content/IT/TXT/?uri=CELEX%3A32010D0087 (permanent copy https://perma.cc/3NWA-4426)

[107] BCR - Binding Corporate Rules, Article 29 Data Protection Working Party, Explanatory Document on the Processor Binding Corporate Rules, http://ec.europa.eu/justice/article-29/documentation/opinion-recommendation/files/2015/wp204.rev_en.pdf (permanent copy https://perma.cc/57LC-NC4D)

Chapter 3.
The Schrems II Judgment

A quick analysis of the complaint that will lead to the second Schrems ruling of the Court of Justice of the Union in July 2018 may suggest a natural evolution of what happened before taking into account the new regulatory environment, characterized by the entry into force of the new European data protection regulation, *GDPR*, and the updated international agreements entered into by Europe and the United States on the overseas transfer of European citizens' data, known as *Privacy Shield.* As explained in more detail in the following pages, the events are profoundly different, with the main difference being the European Union's adoption of a regulation rather than a directive transposed by different member states through national laws.

The regulatory environment

Before analyzing in detail the many changes introduced by the *GDPR* in the processing of personal data, it is worth recalling similarities and differences between directives and regulations. Directive[108] and regulation[109] are both legislative acts issued by the constituent bodies of the institutions with the aim of implementing the objectives set forth in the European Union treaties. *A directive binds the member state to which it is addressed as to the result to be achieved, without prejudice to the competence of national bodies as to form and means*[110] . Directives thus set binding objectives for member states, but leave them free to choose the most appropriate regulatory route to achieve those objectives through what is called "transposition." For example, Directive 95/46/EC is transposed in Italy by Law 675/96. The regulation, on the other hand, is a binding piece of legislation in all its parts that member states are obliged to comply with[111] . Thus, there is no need for a national transposition

[108] Wikipedia, European Union Directive,
https://it.wikipedia.org/wiki/Direttiva_dell%27Unione_europea
(permanent copy https://perma.cc/3F83-P8WT)

[109] Wikipedia, Regulation of the European Union,
https://it.wikipedia.org/wiki/Regolamento_dell%27Unione_europea
(permanent copy https://perma.cc/MF88-3L3T)

[110] Treaty on the Functioning of the European Union, Article 288 (formerly Article 249 TEC),
https://eur-lex.europa.eu/legal-content/IT/TXT/?uri=CELEX:12012E/TXT
(permanent copy https://perma.cc/A8NQ-AHYY)

[111] Treaty on the Functioning of the European Union, Article 289,
https://eur-lex.europa.eu/legal-content/IT/TXT/?uri=CELEX:12012E/TXT
(permanent copy https://perma.cc/A8NQ-AHYY)

measure, since the regulation is immediately binding and obligatory towards all entities, public or private, obliged to comply with European Union law.

Regulation (EU) 2016/679[112] of the European Parliament and of the Council of April 27, 2016, *on the protection of individuals with regard to the processing of personal data and on the free movement of such data and repealing Directive 95/46/EC (General Data Protection Regulation)*, is published in the Official Journal of the European Union L 119/1 on May 4, 2016, enters into force on May 25 of the same year, and applies as of May 25, 2018.

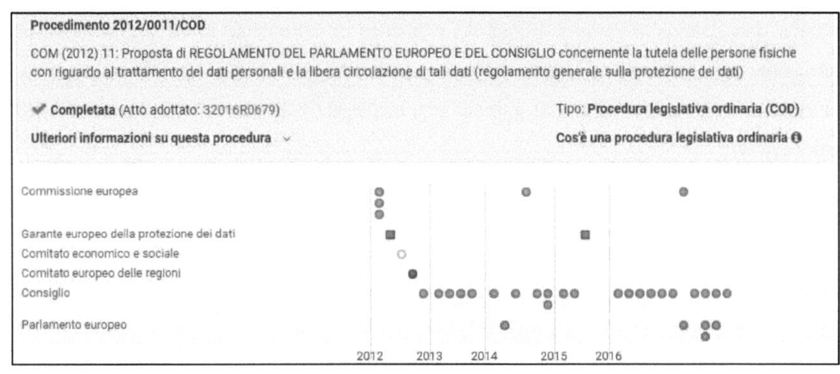

Figure 7 - Regulation (EU) 2016/679 approval process.[113]

It consists of one hundred and seventy-three recitals and ninety-nine articles and has as its first objective to avoid the fragmentation manifested in the transposition of Directive 95/46/EC by the Member States in favor of a scenario in which rights and duties are guaranteed homogeneously in all the States of the Union as stated in Recital 9, "*Although its objectives and principles still remain valid, Directive 95/46/EC has not prevented the fragmentation of the application of personal data protection in the territory of the Union, nor has it eliminated legal uncertainty or the widely held public perception that online operations*

[112] Regulation (EU) 2016/679 of the European Parliament and of the Council of 27 April 2016 on the protection of individuals with regard to the processing of personal data and on the free movement of such data and repealing Directive 95/46/EC (General Data Protection Regulation), https://eur-lex.europa.eu/legal-content/IT/TXT/?uri=CELEX%3A32016R0679 (permanent copy https://perma.cc/UB9M-KSHU)

[113] Ordinary legislative procedure 2012/0011/COD on the Proposal for a Regulation of the European Parliament and of the Council on the protection of individuals with regard to the processing of personal data and on the free movement of such data (General Data Protection Regulation), https://eur-lex.europa.eu/legal-content/IT/HIS/?uri=CELEX:32016R0679 (permanent copy https://perma.cc/2CVW-W65Z)

in particular pose risks to the protection of individuals. The coexistence of different levels of protection of the rights and freedoms of natural persons, particularly the right to protection of personal data, with regard to the processing of such data in the member states may hinder the free movement of personal data within the Union. Such differences can therefore constitute an obstacle to the exercise of economic activities on a Union scale, distort competition and prevent national authorities from fulfilling their obligations under Union law. This gap created in levels of protection is due to divergences in the implementation and application of Directive 95/46/EC," and in Recital 10, "*In order to ensure a consistent and high level of protection for natural persons and to remove obstacles to the movement of personal data within the Union, the level of protection of the rights and freedoms of natural persons with regard to the processing of such data should be equivalent in all Member States. Consistent and homogeneous application of the rules protecting the fundamental rights and freedoms of natural persons with regard to the processing of personal data should be ensured throughout the Union.*"

Articles 1 to 4 of Chapter I, *General Provisions*, open the articles with a description of the subject matter, purpose, material[114] and territorial scope, and definitions useful for the proper understanding of the regulation.

Article 1 specifies that the regulation "*lays down rules relating to the protection of natural persons with regard to the processing of personal data, as well as rules relating to the free movement of such* data"[115] and "*protects the fundamental rights and freedoms of natural persons, in particular the right to the protection of* personal *data*"[116] with an obvious reference to the principles of the Charter of Fundamental Rights of the European Union[117] , the Treaty on the Functioning of the European Union[118] and Directive 95/46/EC also cited in

[114] GDPR, Article 2 - Material Scope, Paragraph 1: This Regulation applies to the wholly or partly automated processing of personal data and to the non-automated processing of personal data contained in or intended to be contained in a filing system,
https://gdpr-text.com/it/read/article-2/#para_gdpr-a-02_1
(permanent copy https://perma.cc/ALD9-YSM2)

[115] GDPR, Article 1-Subject and Purpose, Paragraph 1,
https://gdpr-text.com/it/read/article-1/#para_gdpr-a-01_1
(permanent copy https://perma.cc/QD8Z-BFD2)

[116] GDPR, Article 1-Subject and Purpose, paragraph 2,
https://gdpr-text.com/it/read/article-1/#para_gdpr-a-01_2
(permanent copy https://perma.cc/9T7R-33FK)

[117] Charter of Fundamental Rights of the European Union, Article 8 - Protection of Personal Data,
https://www.europarl.europa.eu/charter/pdf/text_it.pdf
(permanent copy https://perma.cc/E4QG-VVMB)

[118] Treaty on the Functioning of the European Union, Article 16 (formerly Article 286 TEC),
https://eur-lex.europa.eu/legal-content/IT/TXT/?uri=CELEX:12012E/TXT
(permanent copy https://perma.cc/A8NQ-AHYY)

recitals 1 to 3. The need to ensure the protection of personal data is also dictated by the particular historical and technological context as stated in Recital 6, "*The rapid pace of technological change and globalization bring new challenges for the protection of personal data. The scale of sharing and collection of personal data has increased significantly. Today's technology enables both private companies and public authorities to use personal data, as never before, in the course of their activities. Increasingly, individuals are making personal information about themselves available to the public on a global scale. Technology has transformed the economy and social relations and should facilitate even more the free movement of personal data within the Union and their transfer to third countries and international organizations, while ensuring a high level of personal data protection.*" The territorial scope, as stated in Article 3, shows the legislator's desire to define a regulation that also fits the globalized reality of large *hi-tech* companies: the regulation "*shall apply to the processing of personal data carried out in the context of the activities of an establishment by a controller or processor in the Union, whether or not the processing is carried out in the* Union."[119] and "*shall apply to the processing of personal data of data subjects located in the Union , carried out by a controller or processor who is not established in the Union, where the processing activities relate to the offering of goods or the provision of services to the said data subjects in the Union, whether or not the* data *subject's payment is compulsory.*"[120] . Chapter I ends with a number of definitions useful for the correct interpretation of the text, including: personal data[121] , processing[122] , profiling , controller[123124] , controller[125] , consent of the data subject[126] , personal data breach[127] , binding corporate rules[128] .

[119] GDPR, Article 3 - Territorial Scope of Application, para, *https://gdpr-text.com/it/read/article-3/#para_gdpr-a-03_1* (permanent copy https://perma.cc/SZ7R-ND3P)

[120] GDPR, Article 3 - Territorial scope, paragraph 2(a), *https://gdpr-text.com/it/read/article-3/#para_gdpr-a-03_2a* (permanent copy https://perma.cc/4ANT-ZQ3C)

[121] GDPR, Article 4 - Definitions, Paragraph 1, "personal data" means any information relating to an identified or identifiable natural person ("data subject"); an identifiable person is one who can be identified, directly or indirectly, by reference in particular to an identifier such as a name, an identification number, location data, an online identifier, or to one or more characteristic features of his or her physical, physiological, genetic, mental, economic, cultural, or social identity, *https://gdpr-text.com/it/read/article-4/#para_gdpr-a-004_1-01* (permanent copy https://perma.cc/G5C4-QF87)

[122] GDPR, Article 4 - Definitions, Paragraph 2, "processing" means any operation or set of operations which is performed upon personal data or sets of personal data, whether or not by automated means, such as collection, recording, organization, structuring, storage, adaptation or alteration, retrieval, consultation, use, disclosure by transmission, dissemination or otherwise making available, alignment or combination, restriction, erasure or destruction, *https://gdpr-text.com/it/read/article-4/#para_gdpr-a-004_1-02* (permanent copy https://perma.cc/PW93-LKHJ)

[123] GDPR, Article 4 - Definitions, Paragraph 4, "profiling" means any form of automated processing of personal

Article 5 opens Chapter II, *Principles*, by outlining the thinking behind the new regulation. Personal data must be "*processed lawfully, fairly and transparently with regard to the* data subject"[129] , who must be informed in clear and simple language about the manner and purpose of the processing. The processing of the data must then be limited to the purposes[130] for which it is collected and kept for a time not exceeding the achievement of the purposes[131] . The same article also introduces a key concept of the regulation: the principle of *accountability*[132] .

---

data consisting of the use of such personal data to evaluate certain personal aspects relating to a natural person, in particular to analyze or predict aspects of that natural person's job performance, economic situation, health, personal preferences, interests, reliability, behavior, location, or movements,
https://gdpr-text.com/it/read/article-4/#para_gdpr-a-004_1-04
(permanent copy https://perma.cc/D6RT-6DSX)

124 GDPR, Article 4 - Definitions, paragraph 7, Data controller" means the natural or legal person, public authority, service or other body which alone or jointly with others determines the purposes and means of the processing of personal data; [...],
https://gdpr-text.com/it/read/article-4/#para_gdpr-a-004_1-07
(permanent copy https://perma.cc/F7RW-3Z54)

125 GDPR, Article 4 - Definitions, paragraph 8, "controller" means the natural or legal person, public authority, service or other body that processes personal data on behalf of the controller,
https://gdpr-text.com/it/read/article-4/#para_gdpr-a-004_1-08
(permanent copy https://perma.cc/7UVJ-SEXJ)

126 GDPR, Article 4 - Definitions, Paragraph 11, "consent of the data subject" means any freely given, specific, informed and unambiguous indication of the data subject's wishes, by which the data subject indicates his or her assent, by way of a statement or unambiguous affirmative action, that personal data relating to him or her be processed,
https://gdpr-text.com/it/read/article-4/#para_gdpr-a-04_1-11
(permanent copy https://perma.cc/W9UU-CBGK)

127 GDPR, Article 4 - Definitions, paragraph 12, "personal data breach" means a security breach that accidentally or unlawfully results in the destruction, loss, alteration, unauthorized disclosure of or access to personal data transmitted, stored or otherwise processed,
https://gdpr-text.com/it/read/article-4/#para_gdpr-a-04_1-12
(permanent copy https://perma.cc/QX32-WPYG)

128 GDPR, Article 4 - Definitions, Paragraph 20, "Binding Corporate Rules" means the personal data protection policies applied by a controller or processor established in the territory of a member state to the transfer or set of transfers of personal data to a controller or processor in one or more third countries, as part of a business group or group of companies carrying out a common economic activity,
https://gdpr-text.com/it/read/article-4/#para_gdpr-a-04_1-20
(permanent copy https://perma.cc/5GXP-2WET)

129 GDPR, Article 5 - Principles applicable to the processing of personal data, paragraph 1(a),
https://gdpr-text.com/it/read/article-5/#para_gdpr-a-05_1a
(permanent copy https://perma.cc/9EBC-258S)

130 GDPR, Article 5 - Principles applicable to the processing of personal data, para. 1(c),
https://gdpr-text.com/it/read/article-5/#para_gdpr-a-05_1c
(permanent copy https://perma.cc/DC8F-66K3)

131 GDPR, Article 5 - Principles applicable to the processing of personal data, paragraph 1(e),
https://gdpr-text.com/it/read/article-5/#para_gdpr-a-05_1e
(permanent copy https://perma.cc/K4B5-JHJX)

132 GDPR, Article 5 - Principles applicable to the processing of personal data, paragraph 2, the controller is responsible for compliance with paragraph 1 and able to prove it ("accountability"),
https://gdpr-text.com/it/read/article-5/#para_gdpr-a-05_2,
(permanent copy https://perma.cc/856F-DGKS)

Article 6, lawfulness *of processing*, specifies that processing is lawful if the data subject has given consent for one or more specific purposes[133] or when it is necessary for the performance of a contract[134] , to fulfill a legal obligation[135] , to safeguard vital interests[136] , to perform a task in the public interest[137] or for a legitimate interest of the data controller provided that the interests, fundamental rights and freedoms do not prevail[138] . The same article in the fourth paragraph[139] specifies that processing for a purpose other than that for which the data was collected, and for which the data subject has therefore not provided consent, is subject to a compatibility check by the data controller as the sole controller: the controller will have to verify whether the new processing is included in the notice signed by the data subject, submit a new notice to request consent for further processing, or apply appropriate encryption, anonymization[140] or pseudonymization[141] safeguards as in the case, for example, of statistical analysis.

The importance of consent on the part of the data subject is thus apparent, and the regulation devotes Article 7, *Conditions for Consent,* to this issue: the request for consent must be "*presented in a way that is clearly distinguishable from other matters, in a comprehensible and easily accessible form, using simple and* clear *language.*"[142] , consent must be able to be

---

[133] GDPR, Article 6 - Lawfulness of Processing, paragraph 1(a), *https://gdpr-text.com/it/read/article-6/#para_gdpr-a-06_1-1a* (permanent copy https://perma.cc/5YHK-SGMN)

[134] GDPR, Article 6 - Lawfulness of Processing, paragraph 1(b), *https://gdpr-text.com/it/read/article-6/#para_gdpr-a-06_1-1b* (permanent copy https://perma.cc/56GV-57B7)

[135] GDPR, Article 6 - Lawfulness of Processing, paragraph 1(c), *https://gdpr-text.com/it/read/article-6/#para_gdpr-a-06_1-1c* (permanent copy https://perma.cc/Y4C2-3Q7Z)

[136] GDPR, Article 6 - Lawfulness of Processing, Paragraph 1(d), *https://gdpr-text.com/it/read/article-6/#para_gdpr-a-06_1-1d* (permanent copy https://perma.cc/N94M-9BX8)

[137] GDPR, Article 6 - Lawfulness of Processing, paragraph 1 (e), *https://gdpr-text.com/it/read/article-6/#para_gdpr-a-06_1-1e* (permanent copy https://perma.cc/K9YP-PQ4V)

[138] GDPR, Article 6 - Lawfulness of Processing, Paragraph 1 (f), *https://gdpr-text.com/it/read/article-6/#para_gdpr-a-06_1-1f* (permanent copy https://perma.cc/FJC9-XUTF)

[139] GDPR, Article 6 - Lawfulness of processing, paragraph 4, *https://gdpr-text.com/it/read/article-6/#para_gdpr-a-06_4* (permanent copy https://perma.cc/J3XL-ZDMB)

[140] Wikipedia, Data anonymization, *https://en.wikipedia.org/wiki/Data_anonymization* (permanent copy https://perma.cc/JZD3-XQ84)

[141] Wikipedia, Pseudonymization, *https://en.wikipedia.org/wiki/Pseudonymization* (permanent copy https://perma.cc/QK4V-7EAY)

[142] GDPR, Article 7 - Conditions for consent, paragraph 2, *https://gdpr-text.com/it/read/article-7/#para_gdpr-a-07_2* (permanent copy https://perma.cc/3WVK-WXLG)

"*withdrawn as easily as it is* given."[143] , consent is not freely given if "*the performance of a contract, including the provision of a service, is conditional on the provision of consent to the processing of personal data not necessary for the performance of that* contract."[144] .

The remaining articles of Chapter II are of no particular interest in relation to the topics covered in this paper: article 8, *conditions applicable to the consent of minors in relation to information society services*; article 9, *processing of special categories of personal data*; article 10, *processing of personal data relating to criminal convictions and offenses*; and article 11, *processing that does not require identification.*

Chapter III is devoted to the rights of the data subject. Article 12, *Transparent information, communication and modalities for the exercise of the data subject's rights*, requires the data controller to "*provide the data subject with all information [...] and communication [...] relating to the processing in a concise, transparent, intelligible and easily accessible form, in* plain *and* intelligible *language.*"[145] . The same article provides that this information may be "*provided in combination with standardized icons to give, in an easily visible, intelligible and clearly legible manner, an overview of the* intended *processing.* "[146] as a further guarantee of transparency of the disclosure. Article 13, information *to be provided where personal data are collected from the data subject*, specifies the information to be provided within the notice such as, for example, the identity of the data controller, the contact details of the data protection officer, the purposes of the processing, the retention period, and, of particular interest to the topics covered in this paper, "*where applicable, the intention of the data controller to transfer personal data to a third country or international organization and the existence or absence of a Commission adequacy decision or [...] reference to appropriate or adequate safeguards and the means of obtaining a copy of such data or the place where they have been made* available."[147] . Article 14, *information to be provided where personal data*

---

143 GDPR, Article 7 - Conditions for consent, paragraph 3, *https://gdpr-text.com/it/read/article-7/#para_gdpr-a-07_3* (permanent copy https://perma.cc/3NPM-43H5)

144 GDPR, Article 7 - Conditions for consent, paragraph 4, *https://gdpr-text.com/it/read/article-7/#para_gdpr-a-07_4* (permanent copy https://perma.cc/A9K5-552Y)

145 GDPR, Article 11 - Processing that does not require identification, para, *https://gdpr-text.com/it/read/article-12/#para_gdpr-a-12_1* (permanent copy https://perma.cc/9JHE-J7UM)

146 GDPR, Article 11 - Processing that does not require identification, paragraph 1(7), *https://gdpr-text.com/it/read/article-12/#para_gdpr-a-12_7* (permanent copy https://perma.cc/ZU6L-ZEBX)

147 GDPR, Article 13 - Information to be provided if personal data is collected from the data subject, paragraph 1 (f), *https://gdpr-text.com/it/read/article-13/#para_gdpr-a-13_1f*

have not been obtained from the data subject, provides similar guidance to the previous article and specifies the obligation of the data controller to provide information to the data subject regarding "*the source from which the personal data originate and, where appropriate, whether the data originate from* publicly *available sources.*"[148] . The following articles detail the rights granted to the data subject: Article 15, *data subject's right of access*[149] , Article 16, right to *rectification*, Article 17, *right to erasure ("right to be forgotten")*, Article 18, *right to restriction of processing*, Article 19, *obligation to notify in case of rectification or erasure of personal data or restriction of processing*[150] , Article 20, *right to data portability*[151] , Article 21, *right to object*[152] , Article 22, *automated decision making concerning natural persons, including profiling*[153] , Article 23, *limitations*[154] .

(permanent copy https://perma.cc/F3MM-FBA9)

148 GDPR, Article 14 - Information to be provided if personal data has not been obtained from the data subject, paragraph 2 (f),
https://gdpr-text.com/it/read/article-14/#para_gdpr-a-14_2f
(permanent copy https://perma.cc/4NEP-NLM8)

149 GDPR, Article 15 - Data Subject's Access Rights, the data subject has the right to obtain from the controller confirmation as to whether or not personal data relating to him or her are being processed [...], to be informed of the existence of appropriate safeguards in the case of transfers to a third country or international organization [...], to obtain a copy of the personal data undergoing processing,
https://gdpr-text.com/it/read/article-15/
(permanent copy https://perma.cc/9LCT-ZR5H)

150 GDPR, Article 19 - Obligation to notify in case of rectification or erasure of personal data or restriction of processing, the data controller shall notify each of the recipients to whom the personal data have been transmitted of any rectification or erasure or restriction of processing,
https://gdpr-text.com/it/read/article-19/#para_gdpr-a-19
(permanent copy https://perma.cc/RW4Y-WHRK)

151 GDPR, Article 20 - Right to Data Portability, para. 1, the data subject has the right to receive in a structured, commonly used and machine-readable format personal data concerning him or her that has been provided to a data controller and has the right to transmit such data to another data controller without hindrance from the controller,
https://gdpr-text.com/it/read/article-20/#para_gdpr-a-20_1
(permanent copy https://perma.cc/RZP2-Y9GS)

152 GDPR, Article 21 - Right to object, paragraph 1, the data subject has the right to object at any time [...] to the processing of personal data concerning him or her,
https://gdpr-text.com/it/read/article-21/#para_gdpr-a-21_1
(permanent copy https://perma.cc/R29S-TTNN)

153 GDPR, Article 22 - Automated Decision Making Regarding Natural Persons, Including Profiling, paragraph 1, a data subject has the right not to be subjected to a decision based solely on automated processing, including profiling, which produces legal effects concerning him or her or affects him or her in a similar significant way,
https://gdpr-text.com/it/read/article-22/#para_gdpr-a-22_1
(permanent copy https://perma.cc/428K-CXZK)

154 GDPR, Article 23 - Limitations, paragraph 1, the law of the Union or of the Member State to which the controller or processor is subject may limit, by means of legislative measures, the scope of the obligations and rights referred to in Articles 12 to 22 [...] where such limitation respects the essence of fundamental rights and freedoms and is a necessary and proportionate measure in a democratic society,
https://gdpr-text.com/it/read/article-23/#para_gdpr-a-23_1
(permanent copy https://perma.cc/F97P-LKJR)

Chapter IV is devoted to the controller and the processor. The first section, *General Obligations*, opens by recalling the principles of *accountability*[155] , *privacy by design* and *privacy by default*[156] to continue by recalling the new actors introduced by the regulation. As specified in Article 4(8), the controller is the natural or legal person, public authority, service or other body that, individually or jointly with others, determines the purposes and means of the processing of personal data therefore this figure is designated on the basis of the position that the person occupies in the entity or company and not on the basis of the relevant competence. For this reason, the legislature has provided for a professional figure specialized in data processing: the data controller or *data processor* i.e., "*the natural or legal person, public authority, service or other body that processes personal data on behalf of the* data *controller.*"[157] .

Article 27, representatives of controllers *or processors not established in the Union*, specifies the obligation to designate in writing a representative in the Union where the controller is not established in the Union and the activities relate to the offering of goods or provision of services for data subjects located in the Union[158] . The same article specifies that "*the representative shall be established in one of the member states where the data subjects are located and whose personal data are* processed"[159] and "*shall be mandated by the controller or processor to act as an interlocutor, in addition to or instead of the controller or processor, in particular supervisory authorities and data subjects, for all matters concerning the* processing."[160] . Article 30, *Registers of Processing Activities*, on the basis of recital 82[161] ,

---

155 GDPR, Article 24 - Subject matter and purpose, paragraph 1, the controller shall implement appropriate technical and organizational measures to ensure, and be able to demonstrate, that processing is carried out in accordance with the regulation,
https://gdpr-text.com/it/read/article-24/#para_gdpr-a-24_1
(permanent copy https://perma.cc/EBP5-Y5V7)

156 GDPR, Article 25 - Data protection by design and protection by default,
https://gdpr-text.com/it/read/article-25/
(permanent copy https://perma.cc/SNX3-7ZA2)

157 GDPR, Article 4 - Definitions, paragraph 8,
https://gdpr-text.com/it/read/article-4/#para_gdpr-a-004_1-08
(permanent copy https://perma.cc/7UVJ-SEXJ)

158 GDPR, Article 3 - Territorial scope, paragraph 2,
https://gdpr-text.com/it/read/article-3/#para_gdpr-a-03_2
(permanent copy https://perma.cc/8KUH-DBDJ)

159 GDPR, Article 27 - Representatives of data controllers or processors not established in the Union, paragraph 3,
https://gdpr-text.com/it/read/article-27/#para_gdpr-a-27_3
(permanent copy https://perma.cc/NB56-MJSV)

160 GDPR, Article 28 - Data controller, paragraph 4,
https://gdpr-text.com/it/read/article-27/#para_gdpr-a-27_4
(permanent copy https://perma.cc/2QCR-3LTN)

161 The controller or processor should keep a record of processing activities carried out under its responsibility

provides for the keeping of a register, by the data controller or its representative, of the processing activities carried out stating the purposes[162] , a description of the categories of data subjects and personal data[163] , recipients[164] , transfers to a third country or international organization[165] , the time limits provided for the deletion of the different categories of data[166] , technical and organizational security measures[167] .

The second section of Chapter IV, *personal data security*, is devoted to "*appropriate technical and organizational measures to ensure a level of security appropriate to the* risk"[168] : pseudonymization and encryption of personal data, but also procedures to ensure confidentiality, integrity, availability and resilience of systems. In the event of a personal data breach, notification to the competent supervisory authority is required[169] and, if it is likely to present a high risk to the rights and freedoms of natural persons, also to the data subject[170] .

162 GDPR, Article 30 - Records of processing activities, paragraph 1(b), *https://gdpr-text.com/it/read/article-30/#para_gdpr-a-30_1b* (permanent copy https://perma.cc/4LDK-XD62)

163 GDPR, Article 30 - Records of processing activities, paragraph 1(c), *https://gdpr-text.com/it/read/article-30/#para_gdpr-a-30_1c* (permanent copy https://perma.cc/L6NC-BXML)

164 GDPR, Article 30 - Records of Processing Activities, paragraph 1(d), the categories of recipients to whom personal data have been or will be disclosed, including recipients in third countries or international organizations, https://gdpr-text.com/it/read/article-30/#para_gdpr-a-30_1d, (permanent copy https://perma.cc/TE5W-TC62)

165 GDPR, Article 30 - Records of Processing Activities, paragraph 1(e), transfers of personal data to a third country or international organization, including identification of the third country or international organization and [...] documentation of appropriate safeguards, https://gdpr-text.com/it/read/article-30/#para_gdpr-a-30_1e, (permanent copy https://perma.cc/L6CS-FP25)

166 GDPR, Article 30 - Records of processing activities, paragraph 1 (f), *https://gdpr-text.com/it/read/article-30/#para_gdpr-a-30_1f* (permanent copy https://perma.cc/7YB4-W2MS)

167 GDPR, Article 30 - Records of processing activities, paragraph 1(g), *https://gdpr-text.com/it/read/article-30/#para_gdpr-a-30_1g* (permanent copy https://perma.cc/LB4E-B2GA)

168 GDPR, Article 32 - Security of Processing, *https://gdpr-text.com/it/read/article-32/* (permanent copy https://perma.cc/8AYY-UJE6)

169 GDPR, Article 33 - Notification of a personal data breach to the supervisory authority, in the event of a personal data breach, the data controller shall notify the competent supervisory authority [...] without undue delay and, where feasible, within 72 hours of becoming aware of it, unless the personal data breach is unlikely to present a risk to the rights and freedoms of natural persons, https://gdpr-text.com/it/read/article-33/, (permanent copy https://perma.cc/GUB3-ZX9H)

170 GDPR, Article 34 - Notification of a personal data breach to the data subject, when the personal data breach is likely to present a high risk to the rights and freedoms of natural persons, the controller shall notify the data subject of the breach without undue delay [...] in plain and intelligible language, https://gdpr-text.com/it/read/article-34/, (permanent copy https://perma.cc/36A2-C9EY)

The third section of Chapter IV, *Data Protection Impact Assessment and Prior Consultation*, focuses attention on processing operations that can be expected to pose a high risk to the rights and freedoms of natural persons, particularly when the use of new technologies is envisaged that, through systematic and comprehensive processing of personal aspects, can, for example, result in profiling on which decisions with legal or otherwise significant effects are based.

The fourth section of Chapter IV, *data protection officer*, is devoted to one of the main new features introduced by the regulation: the *data protection officer*, also known by the acronym *DPO.* This person is designated by the data controller and data processor "on the *basis of professional qualities, in particular specialized knowledge of data protection law and practice*,"[171] and is responsible for informing and advising on obligations under the regulation, overseeing compliance with the regulation through awareness-raising and training of staff involved in processing, providing advice on impact assessment, and acting as a point of contact for processing issues[172] .

The fifth and final section of Chapter IV, *Codes of Conduct and Certification*, aims to encourage "*the development of codes of conduct intended to contribute to the proper application of the* Regulation"[173] and "*the establishment of data protection certification mechanisms for the purpose of demonstrating compliance of processing operations* carried out."[174] . Codes of conduct drawn up by associations and other bodies representing categories of data controllers or processors may specify how the regulation is to be applied with regard to the lawfulness and transparency of processing, legitimate interests pursued, information provided to the public and data subjects, exercise of data subjects' rights, security measures, and transfer to third countries or international organizations. Codes of conduct are submitted

---

171 GDPR, Article 37 - Designation of the data protection officer,
https://gdpr-text.com/it/read/article-37/
(permanent copy https://perma.cc/M6VK-8TUJ)

172 GDPR, Article 39 - Duties of the data protection officer,
https://gdpr-text.com/it/read/article-39/
(permanent copy https://perma.cc/U9MY-LLR6)

173 GDPR, Article 40 - Codes of Conduct, the Member States, supervisory authorities, the Committee and the Commission shall encourage the development of codes of conduct designed to contribute to the proper application of this Regulation, according to the specificities of the various processing sectors and the specific needs of micro, small and medium-sized enterprises,
https://gdpr-text.com/it/read/article-40/,
(permanent copy https://perma.cc/4JHN-CAUN)

174 GDPR, Article 42 - Certification, Member States, supervisory authorities, the Committee and the Commission shall encourage, in particular at the Union level, the establishment of data protection certification mechanisms as well as data protection seals and marks for the purpose of demonstrating compliance with this Regulation of processing operations carried out by data controllers and processors,
https://gdpr-text.com/it/read/article-42/,
(permanent copy https://perma.cc/RQU7-K46R)

to the competent supervisory authority[175] which gives an opinion on compliance with the regulation and, if approved, proceeds to their registration and publication. Certifications, seals and marks, issued by accredited certification bodies[176] , "*in addition to the adherence of data controllers or processors subject to this Regulation, [...] may be established for the purpose of demonstrating the provision of appropriate safeguards by controllers or processors not subject to the regulation in the context of transfers of personal data to third countries or* international *organizations.*"[177] , adherence is "*voluntary and accessible through a* transparent *procedure.*"[178] and "*does not reduce the responsibility of the controller or processor with regard to compliance with the* regulation."[179] .

Chapter V, *transfers of personal data to third countries or international organizations*, is the one of most interest to the topics discussed in this paper.

The principle underlying this type of transfer is summarized in Article 44[180] : "*Any transfer of personal data that are processed or are intended to be processed after transfer to a third country or international organization, including onward transfers of personal data from a third country or international organization to another third country or international organization, shall take place only if the controller and the processor comply with the conditions laid down in this Chapter, subject to the other provisions of this Regulation. All provisions of this Chapter shall be applied in order to ensure that the level of protection of natural persons guaranteed by this Regulation is not undermined.*" The goal of the regulation is thus to ensure a controlled supply chain even for data transferred outside Europe, where any transfer is authorized only where the recipient can provide processing guarantees equivalent

---

[175] GDPR, Article 40 - Codes of Conduct, paragraph 7, where the draft code of conduct relates to processing activities in several member states, prior to approval, the supervisory authority which is competent shall submit it to the committee which shall give an opinion on compliance with the regulation, https://gdpr-text.com/it/read/article-40/#para_gdpr-a-40_7, (permanent copy https://perma.cc/4UR7-YRDZ)

[176] GDPR, Article 43 - Certification Bodies, https://gdpr-text.com/it/read/article-43/, (permanent copy https://perma.cc/ZX5X-USCZ)

[177] GDPR, Article 42 - Certification, paragraph 2, *https://gdpr-text.com/it/read/article-42/#para_gdpr-a-42_2* (permanent copy https://perma.cc/L2RD-47ZH)

[178] GDPR, Article 42 - Certification, paragraph 3, *https://gdpr-text.com/it/read/article-42/#para_gdpr-a-42_3* (permanent copy https://perma.cc/TCN6-VW3N)

[179] GDPR, Article 42 - Certification, paragraph 4, *https://gdpr-text.com/it/read/article-42/#para_gdpr-a-42_4* (permanent copy https://perma.cc/CS3A-6DC6)

[180] GDPR, Article 44- General principle for transfer, https://gdpr-text.com/it/read/article-44/, (permanent copy https://perma.cc/VA2Z-PU9R)

to those specified in the regulation. More precisely, the transfer is authorized on the basis of an adequacy decision by the Commission[181] or in case of adequate guarantees provided directly by the controller or processor[182] .

The Commission's adequacy decision may relate to a third country, a territory or specific sector(s) within the third country, an international organization, and in that case the transfer does not require specific authorization. In assessing the adequacy of the level of protection, the Commission considers several elements including the rule of law, respect for human rights and fundamental freedoms, general and sectoral legislation (e.g., public authorities' access to personal data), effective and enforceable rights of data subjects, and the existence of independent supervisory authorities to ensure compliance[183] . Each adequacy decision is subject to periodic review, at least every four years, with the possibility that it may be revoked, modified or suspended in the absence of adequate safeguards[184] . The list of third countries and international organizations with an adequate level of protection is published by the Commission in the Official Journal of the European Union and on the website[185] .

In the absence of an adequacy decision, the controller or processor may transfer personal data only by providing adequate safeguards and provided that data subjects have enforceable rights and effective remedies. Binding corporate rules, codes of conduct and certifications may constitute adequate safeguards and may not require specific authorization from a supervisory authority[186] . Subject to the authorization of the competent supervisory authority, contractual clauses between the controller or processor and the recipient of personal data in the third

---

181 GDPR, Article 45 - Transfer on the basis of an adequacy decision, https://gdpr-text.com/it/read/article-45/, (permanent copy https://perma.cc/G4JY-Y8BS)

182 GDPR, Article 46 - Transfer subject to adequate safeguards, https://gdpr-text.com/it/read/article-46/, (permanent copy https://perma.cc/9JR6-ANBW)

183 GDPR, Article 45 - Transfer on the basis of an adequacy decision, paragraph 2, *https://gdpr-text.com/it/read/article-45/#para_gdpr-a-45_2* (permanent copy https://perma.cc/RU3Q-HYQL)

184 GDPR, Article 45 - Transfer on the basis of an adequacy decision, paragraph 3, *https://gdpr-text.com/it/read/article-45/#para_gdpr-a-45_3* (permanent copy https://perma.cc/MJ75-EQ57)
GDPR, Article 45 - Transfer on the basis of an adequacy decision, paragraph 5, *https://gdpr-text.com/it/read/article-45/#para_gdpr-a-45_5-1* (permanent copy https://perma.cc/DCL6-7TSU)

185 European Commission, Adequacy decisions, How the EU determines if a non-EU country has an adequate level of data protection, *https://ec.europa.eu/info/law/law-topic/data-protection/international-dimension-data-protection/adequacy-decisions_en* (permanent copy *https://perma.cc/5Y62-9RVG*)

186 GDPR, Article 46 - Transfer subject to adequate safeguards, paragraph 2, *https://gdpr-text.com/it/read/article-46/#para_gdpr-a-46_2* (permanent copy https://perma.cc/69A5-82KP)

country or international organization may also constitute adequate safeguards[187] . Contractual clauses are the subject of the 0.

Article 49, *exceptions in specific situations*, allows transfer in the absence of an adequacy decision or adequate safeguards in cases where the data subject, informed of the possible risks, has explicitly consented to the proposed transfer or in cases where the transfer is necessary for the performance of a contract, for important reasons of public interest, to exercise a right in court, or to protect vital interests. In the absence of these conditions, the transfer is permissible only if it concerns a limited number of data subjects, for the pursuit of compelling legitimate interests of the data controller, limited to a restricted set of personal data, at the direct request of the persons having a legitimate interest and having informed the supervisory authority.

Chapter VI, *Independent Supervisory Authorities*, provides for the establishment of independent public authorities within each member state to supervise the application of the Regulation, protect the fundamental rights and freedoms of natural persons, and facilitate the free movement of personal data within the Union[188] . Each supervisory authority has jurisdiction in the territory of its respective Member State[189] and, in the case of cross-border processing, is competent to act as lead authority if the Member State is the location of the principal or sole establishment of the controller or processor[190] . Each supervisory authority has investigative powers[191] , corrective powers[192] and authorizing and advisory powers[193] .

---

[187] GDPR, Article 46 - Transfer subject to adequate safeguards, paragraph 3,
https://gdpr-text.com/it/read/article-46/#para_gdpr-a-46_3
(permanent copy https://perma.cc/PF45-M2HW)

[188] GDPR, Article 51 - Supervisory Authority,
https://gdpr-text.com/it/read/article-51/
(permanent copy https://perma.cc/CW89-726U)
GDPR, Article 52 - Independence,
https://gdpr-text.com/it/read/article-52/
(permanent copy https://perma.cc/AK64-QP49)

[189] GDPR, Article 55 - Competence,
https://gdpr-text.com/it/read/article-55/
(permanent copy https://perma.cc/E6ZN-VA2J)

[190] GDPR, Article 56 - Competence of the lead supervisory authority,
https://gdpr-text.com/it/read/article-56/
(permanent copy https://perma.cc/8UAQ-GND5)

[191] GDPR, Article 58 - Powers, paragraph 1,
https://gdpr-text.com/it/read/article-58/#para_gdpr-a-58_1
(permanent copy https://perma.cc/H4MM-EBZN)

[192] GDPR, Article 58 - Powers, paragraph 2,
https://gdpr-text.com/it/read/article-58/#para_gdpr-a-58_2
(permanent copy https://perma.cc/648W-SASZ)

[193] GDPR, Article 58 - Powers, paragraph 3,
https://gdpr-text.com/it/read/article-58/#para_gdpr-a-58_3
(permanent copy https://perma.cc/8MHH-C4HG)

Among the remedial powers, it is interesting to mention the possibility of issuing warnings that the planned processing operations are likely to violate the regulation, issuing warnings where the processing operations have violated the regulation, ordering the controller to comply with the data subject's requests, ordering the controller to bring the processing operations into conformity with the regulation, imposing a temporary or definitive restriction on processing, ordering the rectification or erasure of personal data, revoking a certification, imposing an administrative fine, and ordering the suspension of data flows to a third-country recipient or an international organization.

Chapter VII, *Cooperation and Consistency*, based on Recitals 124, 125, 126, 127, 130 and 131, prepares rules for cooperation and coordination among member states' supervisory authorities with the aim of ensuring uniform application of the regulation in all territories of the Union.

The first section, cooperation, is devoted to cooperation between the lead supervisory authority and other supervisory authorities in cases of cross-border processing[194] , mutual assistance in fulfilling their tasks[195] and joint operations such as investigations and law enforcement[196] .

The second section, *coherence*, aims to contribute to the uniform application of the regulation throughout the Union[197] , ensure the involvement of all supervisory authorities in matters of general application or having effects in more than one state[198] , settle disputes between

[194] GDPR, Article 60 - Cooperation between the lead supervisory authority and other supervisory authorities concerned,
https://gdpr-text.com/it/read/article-60/,
(permanent copy https://perma.cc/N66R-3MY2)

[195] GDPR, Article 61 - Mutual Assistance,
https://gdpr-text.com/it/read/article-61/
(permanent copy https://perma.cc/6ZVB-WE6K)

[196] GDPR, Article 62 - Joint operations of supervisory authorities,
https://gdpr-text.com/it/read/article-62/
(permanent copy https://perma.cc/Q35H-HAXN)

[197] GDPR, Article 63 - Consistency Mechanism,
https://gdpr-text.com/it/read/article-63/
(permanent copy https://perma.cc/46YF-MGFU)

[198] GDPR, Article 64 - Opinion of the European Data Protection Board,
https://gdpr-text.com/it/read/article-64/
(permanent copy https://perma.cc/RH6A-5RBX)

supervisory authorities[199] , and provide for the immediate adoption of non-agreed interim measures in the case of exceptional circumstances[200] .

The third section, the *European Data Protection Board*, establishes a Union body with legal personality consisting of a senior figure from a supervisory authority for each member state and the European Data Protection Supervisor[201] . The Commission has the right to participate in the activities and meetings of the committee but without voting rights. The committee operates with independence[202] and is responsible for ensuring the consistent application of the regulation[203] .

Chapter VIII, *Remedies, Liability and Sanctions*, specifies that "a *data subject who considers that the processing operations concerning him or her are in breach of this Regulation shall have the right to lodge a complaint with a supervisory authority, in particular in the Member State in which he or she normally resides, works, or of the place where the alleged* breach *occurred.*"[204] and "*shall have the right to mandate a non-profit body, organization or association, [.] whose statutory objectives are in the public interest and who are active in the field of the protection of the rights and freedoms of data subjects with regard to the protection of personal data, to bring the complaint on his behalf and to exercise on his behalf the rights [...] as well as, if provided for by the law of the Member States, the right to obtain* compensation."[205] . Article 83, *General Conditions for Imposing Administrative Sanctions*, provides for the imposition of administrative pecuniary sanctions of up to twenty million euros, or for enterprises, up to 4 percent of total annual worldwide turnover, whichever is

---

199 GDPR, Article 65 - Dispute resolution by the committee, *https://gdpr-text.com/it/read/article-65/* (permanent copy https://perma.cc/L9DS-PVWD)

200 GDPR, Article 66 - Emergency Procedure, *https://gdpr-text.com/it/read/article-66/* (permanent copy https://perma.cc/2WFN-CB5Z)

201 GDPR, Article 68 - European Data Protection Board, *https://gdpr-text.com/it/read/article-68/* (permanent copy https://perma.cc/T4V2-ZSFK)

202 GDPR; Article 69 - Independence, *https://gdpr-text.com/it/read/article-69/* (permanent copy https://perma.cc/KV9K-S62Q)

203 GDPR; Article 70 - Duties of the committee, *https://gdpr-text.com/it/read/article-70/* (permanent copy https://perma.cc/8LAY-VKYU)

204 GDPR; Article 77 - Right to lodge a complaint with the supervisory authority, *https://gdpr-text.com/it/read/article-77/* (permanent copy https://perma.cc/38L9-WDVE)

205 GDPR; Article 80 - Representation of data subjects, *https://gdpr-text.com/it/read/article-80/* (permanent copy https://perma.cc/3K35-LA4R)

higher, in the event of violation of the provisions[206] or failure to comply with an order by the supervisory authority[207] .

Chapter IX, *Provisions on Specific Processing Situations*, is devoted to specific types of processing that are of little interest with respect to the topics discussed in this paper: freedom of expression and information[208] , public access to official documents[209] , national identification number[210] (or any other means of identification in general use), data in the context of labor relations[211] , processing for archiving purposes in the public interest, scientific or historical research, or statistical purposes[212] .

Chapter X, *Delegated and Implementing Acts*, recalling what is expressed in recital 166, delegates to the Commission the power to adopt acts in accordance with Article 290 of the Treaty on the Functioning of the European Union, in particular delegated acts concerning the criteria and requirements for certification mechanisms, the information to be presented in the form of standardized icons, and the procedures for providing such icons.

The last chapter, *final provisions*, specifies the entry into force of the regulation as of May 25, 2016 and its application as of May 25, 2018[213] resulting in the repeal of Directive 95/46/EC[214].

---

206 GDPR; Article 83 - General conditions for imposing administrative fines, paragraph 5, *https://gdpr-text.com/it/read/article-83/#para_gdpr-a-83_5* (permanent copy https://perma.cc/3QFG-TUEH)

207 GDPR; Article 83 - General conditions for imposing administrative pecuniary sanctions, paragraph 6, *https://gdpr-text.com/it/read/article-83/#para_gdpr-a-83_6* (permanent copy https://perma.cc/A2LQ-HQZJ)

208 GDPR; Article 85 - Treatment and Freedom of Expression and Information, *https://gdpr-text.com/it/read/article-85/* (permanent copy https://perma.cc/A5VF-44X7)

209 GDPR; Article 86 - Processing and public access to official documents, *https://gdpr-text.com/it/read/article-86/* (permanent copy https://perma.cc/P87M-JP7K)

210 GDPR; Article 87 - Processing of national identification number, *https://gdpr-text.com/it/read/article-87/* (permanent copy https://perma.cc/RYD4-268H)

211 GDPR; Article 88 - Data processing in the context of labor relations, *https://gdpr-text.com/it/read/article-88/* (permanent copy https://perma.cc/9UHK-A6DY)

212 GDPR; Article 89 - Guarantees and exceptions relating to processing for archiving purposes in the public interest, scientific or historical research, or statistical purposes, *https://gdpr-text.com/it/read/article-89/* (permanent copy https://perma.cc/U3L6-HEM4)

213 GDPR; Article 99 - Entry into force and enforcement, *https://gdpr-text.com/it/read/article-99/* (permanent copy https://perma.cc/3MMF-WHCY)

214 GDPR; Article 94 - Repeal of Directive 95/46/EC, *https://gdpr-text.com/it/read/article-94/* (permanent copy https://perma.cc/HP5X-FHGC)

Also of particular interest are Article 96, *relationship to previously concluded agreements*, where international agreements involving the transfer of personal data to third countries or international organizations concluded before May 24, 2016, remain in force, and Article 97, *committee reports*, which stipulates a review of the regulation by May 25, 2020, and every 4 years thereafter specifically for the transfer of personal data to third countries or international organizations[215] .

Article 95, *Relationship to Directive 2002/58/EC*, recalling when expressed in recital 173, specifies that while the Regulation does not impose additional obligations beyond what is set forth in the aforementioned Directive in relation to processing in the context of the provision of publicly available electronic communications services over public communications networks in the Union, the Directive itself should be reviewed to ensure consistency with the Regulation.

The January 10, 2017 Proposal for a Regulation of the European Parliament and of the Council[216] , *on privacy and the protection of personal data in electronic communications and repealing Directive 2002/58/EC (Regulation on privacy and electronic communications)*, reviews the contents of the directive to ensure consistency with the *GDPR*.

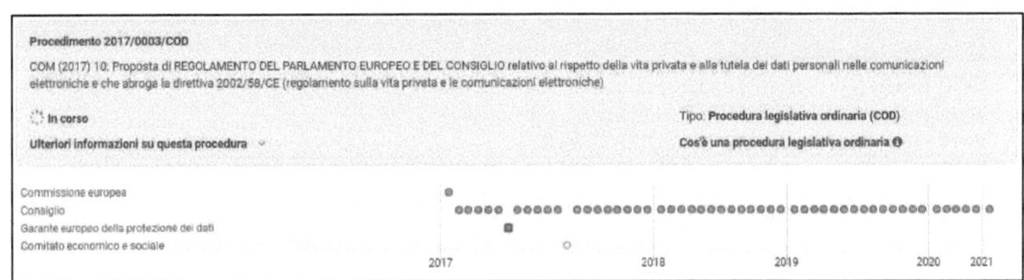

Figure 8 - Proceedings for the repeal of Directive 2002/58/EC[217]

---

[215] GDPR; Article 97 - Commission Reports, paragraph 2 (a), https://gdpr-text.com/it/read/article-97/#para_gdpr-a-97_2a (permanent copy https://perma.cc/JXG4-G5XG)

[216] Proposal for a Regulation of the European Parliament and of the Council on privacy and personal data protection in electronic communications and repealing Directive 2002/58/EC (Regulation on privacy and electronic communications), https://eur-lex.europa.eu/legal-content/IT/ALL/?uri=CELEX:52017PC0010 (permanent copy https://perma.cc/2LY5-67GJ)

[217] Ordinary legislative procedure 2017/0003/COD on the proposal for a Regulation of the European Parliament and of the Council on privacy and personal data protection in electronic communications and repealing Directive 2002/58/EC (Regulation on privacy and electronic communications), https://eur-lex.europa.eu/legal-content/IT/HIS/?uri=CELEX:52017PC0010 (permanent copy https://perma.cc/U4BL-TEMD)

The objectives and principles presided over by the directive remain valid even in the current framework, but the regulatory text does not appear to keep pace with technological development. In particular, the directive gives no indication of so-called over-the-top communication services[218] which therefore remain excluded from it and, instead, must necessarily be included. The Commission's choice to submit a proposal for a regulation is intended to ensure consistency with the *GDPR* and legal certainty vis-à-vis users and businesses by avoiding interpretations during transposition by member states. This will is also demonstrated by the provision of entrusting the monitoring of compliance with the provisions to national authorities already in charge of overseeing the application of the *GDPR*. The proposal, at present, is still under discussion among member states.

Example of the application of Regulation (EU) 2016/679

The Data Protection Authority's order of injunction against the University "Luigi Bocconi" of Milan dated September 16, 2021[219] allows us to analyze multiple aspects of Regulation (EU) 2016/679 in the protection of individuals with regard to the processing of personal data.

The decision of the supervisory authority originates from the complaint filed in late April 2020 by an English student in the Political Science course, Joseph Donat Bolton[220] , regarding possible violations of data protection regulations in connection with the use of a supervisory system, *proctoring*, as part of the written examination tests.

The university, in the context of the epidemiological emergency from *SARS-CoV-2*, identified an alternative way of conducting university examinations at a distance and, with the aim of ensuring the same guarantees provided for in-person examinations, requested students' consent for the processing of special categories of personal data, biometric data, indicating that in the absence of such consent they would not be able to conduct online examinations.

---

218 Over-the-top (OTT) services are those services based on the use of the Internet for the provision of interpersonal communications, almost for example voice-over-IP (VoIP) and instant messaging (IM) services

219 Garante per la Protezione dei Dati Personali, Order of injunction against the Università Commerciale "Luigi Bocconi" of Milan, Register of Measures No. 317 of September 16, 2021, *https://www.garanteprivacy.it/home/docweb/-/docweb-display/docweb/9703988* (permanent copy https://perma.cc/PB4P-AVB2)

220 Open, Joseph, the student who got Bocconi fined for privacy violation: "Without data, no exams." *https://www.open.online/2021/09/30/privacy-universita-bocconi-multa-intervista/* (permanent copy https://perma.cc/66ND-VM6V)

In more detail, the supervision system consists of two modules from the U.S.-based company Respondus Inc.[221] : Lockdown *Browser*[222] is an Internet browsing browser that, by blocking other applications, prevents the student from consulting texts and receiving external help during the exam; Respondus Monitor[223] is a monitoring tool that through the use of camera allows the student to verify the correspondence between the student and the ID and to identify abnormal student behavior, such as looking away from the computer monitor during the exam.

In compliance with the principle of lawfulness, fairness and transparency, the data controller must provide the data subject, before the processing begins, with information in a concise, transparent, intelligible and easily accessible form, with simple and clear language[224] while, in the case at hand, the Data Protection Authority notes the absence of several elements within the information provided to students. This refers to the processing of biometric data and a short list of other personal data, given by way of example and not exhaustively, not mentioning the further specific processing put in place by the Respondus system: the tracking of the student's behavior during the test, subsequent processing by profiling and the audio-video recording of the test. The same notice generically states that personal data are retained as long as necessary for the legitimate purposes of processing without indicating the different retention periods for different categories of personal data and processing purposes. The transfer made to the United States of America is generically stated by the phrase "*personal data will be processed by the Controller within and outside the territory of the European Union*" not specifying the premise of the transfer on the basis of the Implementing Decision (EU) 2016/1250, explained in the following pages, and thus not providing information to students about the third country of destination and the safeguards adopted for the transfer.

The investigative activity of the supervisory authority points out that "*such systems must not be unduly invasive and involve monitoring of the student in excess of the actual needs, since, although the necessary compliance with the rules for the conduct of tests should be*

---

221 Respondus, Assessment Tools for Learning Systems,
https://web.respondus.com/
(permanent copy https://perma.cc/JZ44-X5JB)

222 Respondus, LockDown Browser, Prevent cheating during online exams,
https://web.respondus.com/he/lockdownbrowser/
(permanent copy https://perma.cc/2FAD-TNRN)

223 Respondus, Respondus Monitor, Fully-automated proctoring for online exams,
https://web.respondus.com/he/monitor/
(permanent copy https://perma.cc/5QK6-SK4M)

224 GDPR, Article 12 - Transparent information, communication and modalities for the exercise of data subject's rights,
https://gdpr-text.com/it/read/article-12/
(permanent copy https://perma.cc/AN5S-ZXSD)

guaranteed even online, systems involving electronic surveillance lacking the necessary limits and guarantees cannot be considered acceptable," and notes the unlawfulness of the processing of personal data carried out by the university in particular for failure to comply with the principles of "lawfulness, fairness and transparency"[225] , "data minimization"[226] , "storage limitation"[227] , "privacy by *design*" and "*privacy by* default"[228] , for the processing of biometric data[229] in the absence of an appropriate legal basis, and for the transfer to the United States of America without having verified and ensured effective compliance with the conditions set out in Chapter V of Regulation (EU) 2016/679[230] also in relation to special categories of data. Violation of the provisions thus results in the unusability of the processed personal data.

Pursuant to Article 58(2)(f) of Regulation (EU) 2016/679, the Data Protection Supervisor deems it necessary to "*order the restriction of processing, prohibiting the University from any further processing operations, with regard to the biometric data of students and the data on the basis of which profiling of data subjects is carried out using the Respondus system, and prohibit the transfer of personal data of data subjects to the United States of America, in the absence of adequate safeguards for them.*" The administrative fine imposed under Article 83

---

225 GDPR, Article 5 - Principles applicable to the processing of personal data, paragraph 1(a), *https://gdpr-text.com/it/read/article-5/#para_gdpr-a-05_1a* (permanent copy https://perma.cc/9EBC-258S)
GDPR, Article 6 - Lawfulness of Processing, *https://gdpr-text.com/it/read/article-6/* (permanent copy https://perma.cc/376U-CZB3)

226 GDPR, Article 5 - Principles applicable to the processing of personal data, paragraph 1(c), *https://gdpr-text.com/it/read/article-5/#para_gdpr-a-05_1c* (permanent copy https://perma.cc/DC8F-66K3)

227 GDPR, Article 5 - Principles applicable to the processing of personal data, paragraph 1(e), *https://gdpr-text.com/it/read/article-5/#para_gdpr-a-05_1e* (permanent copy https://perma.cc/K4B5-JHJX)
GDPR, Article 13 - Information to be provided if personal data is collected from the data subject, *https://gdpr-text.com/it/read/article-13/* (permanent copy https://perma.cc/CUY2-J4LQ)

228 GDPR, Article 25 - Data protection by design and protection by default, *https://gdpr-text.com/it/read/article-25/* (permanent copy https://perma.cc/SNX3-7ZA2)

229 GDPR, Article 9 - Processing of special categories of personal data, *https://gdpr-text.com/it/read/article-9/* (permanent copy https://perma.cc/BB7Q-2Z7M)
GDPR, Article 35 - Data Protection Impact Assessment, *https://gdpr-text.com/it/read/article-35/* (permanent copy https://perma.cc/X7VK-YR7J)

230 GDPR, Article 44 - General principle for transfer, *https://gdpr-text.com/it/read/article-44/* (permanent copy https://perma.cc/VA2Z-PU9R)
GDPR, Article 46 - Transfer subject to adequate safeguards, *https://gdpr-text.com/it/read/article-46/* (permanent copy https://perma.cc/9JR6-ANBW)

of Regulation (EU) 2016/679, in connection with the mishandling of data belonging to special categories of more than four thousand students and taking into account the cooperative and well-disposed behavior to incorporate the findings of the supervisory authority, is determined at two hundred thousand euros. Given the particular sensitivity of the data processed, the ancillary sanction of publication of the order on the website of the Data Protection Authority is also applied.

The Privacy Shield

The October 6, 2015 ruling by the Court of Justice of the European Union invalidating Decision 2000/520/EC and annulling the *safe harbor* regime for the transfer of data EU-US leaves in abeyance numerous existing relationships between U.S. and European entities, necessitating the approval of an equivalent agreement but with greater safeguards.

The European Commission and the government of the United States of America begin work on the drafting of the new agreement with the aim of providing more and new safeguards for European citizens, and on February 2, 2016, the European Commission publishes the draft "adequacy decision"[231] , which will be named *Privacy Shield EU-US*, thereby declaring principles of protection deemed equivalent to those offered by existing European legislation: the Directive 95/46/EC.

The European Commission's press note states, "*This agreement will protect the fundamental rights of European citizens should their data be transferred to the United States and provide legal certainty for businesses [...] the new agreement provides stronger obligations for companies in the United States to protect the personal data of European citizens and stronger monitoring and enforcement by the U.S. Department of Commerce and the Federal Trade Commission (FTC), including through increased cooperation with European Data Protection Authorities [...] for the first time ever, the United States has provided binding assurances to the European Union that public authorities' access for national security purposes will be subject to clear limitations, safeguards and control mechanisms [...] the United States has assured that it will not conduct indiscriminate mass surveillance of* European *citizens.*"[232] .

---

[231] European Commission, EU Commission and United States agree on new framework for transatlantic data flows: EU-US Privacy Shield,
https://ec.europa.eu/commission/presscorner/detail/en/IP_16_216
(permanent copy https://perma.cc/N8TN-9P5X)

[232] This new framework will protect the fundamental rights of Europeans where their data is transferred to the United States and ensure legal certainty for businesses [...] the new arrangement will provide stronger

There are three main innovations that are present in the new agreement in order to ensure the effective protection of the rights of European citizens: those who believe that their data has been misused have the possibility to appeal, the European Data Protection Authorities have the possibility to file complaints with the Federal Trade Commission, and finally, an ombudsman, *Ombudsperson*, is in charge of handling complaints about possible access by national *intelligence* authorities. This infographic published in 2016 by the Data Protection Authority summarizes the main changes introduced by the *Privacy Shield.*

---

obligations on companies in the U.S. to protect the personal data of Europeans and stronger monitoring and enforcement by the U.S. Department of Commerce and Federal Trade Commission (FTC), including through increased cooperation with European Data Protection Authorities [...] for the first time ever, the United States has given the EU binding assurances that the access of public authorities for national security purposes will be subject to clear limitations, safeguards and oversight mechanisms [...] the U.S. has assured that it does not conduct mass or indiscriminate surveillance of Europeans

L'accordo detto *Privacy Shield* fra Ue e USA **impone alle imprese americane obblighi più stringenti** di tutela dei dati personali degli europei. E' in linea con quanto chiesto dalla Corte di giustizia dell'Ue, che aveva invalidato il precedente accordo detto «Safe Harbor», ossia «Porto sicuro». Il *Privacy Shield* prevede che le autorità americane **vigilino e assicurino con più forza** sul rispetto dell'accordo e che collaborino in misura maggiore con le Autorità europee per la protezione dei dati. L'accordo contiene - ed è la prima volta - dichiarazioni e impegni assunti formalmente per quanto riguarda **l'accesso ai dati da parte di soggetti dell'Amministrazione americana**.

Gli elementi fondamentali del nuovo accordo

SETTORE COMMERCIALE

Obblighi stringenti per le imprese e rigide misure di attuazione

- Più trasparenza
- Meccanismi di controllo del rispetto delle regole da parte delle imprese
- Sanzioni o esclusione dai benefici dell'accordo per le imprese che non lo rispettano
- Condizioni più rigide per trasferire i dati a destinatari ulteriori

ACCESSO AI DATI DA PARTE DELL'AMMINISTRAZIONE USA

Precise garanzie e obblighi di trasparenza

- Per la prima volta, l'Amministrazione USA ha garantito formalmente che l'accesso delle autorità pubbliche ai dati personali sarà soggetto a limiti, garanzie e meccanismi di controllo specifici e definiti
- Le Autorità USA affermano che non vi saranno attività di sorveglianza indiscriminata o massiva
- Le imprese potranno dichiarare il numero approssimativo di richieste di accesso ricevute
- Disponibile un nuovo strumento di tutela giuridica attraverso il cosiddetto «difensore civico» (*Ombudsperson)* creato per il *Privacy Shield* : un soggetto indipendente incaricato di ricevere e decidere i reclami presentati dagli interessati

STRUMENTI DI TUTELA GIURIDICA

Vi sono diverse possibilità per far valere i propri diritti

- **Rivolgersi direttamente all'impresa**, che deve rispondere, in caso di reclamo da parte di un interessato, entro 45 giorni
- **Utilizzare un meccanismo di ADR** (Risoluzione alternativa delle controversie), gratuito
- **Rivolgersi all'Autorità di protezione dati**, che collaborerà con il *Department of Commerce* e la *Federal Trade Commission* degli USA per garantire accertamenti sui reclami ancora pendenti presentati da cittadini Ue e giungere rapidamente alla loro definizione
- **Rivolgersi al Privacy Shield Panel** (Collegio arbitrale del *Privacy Shield*) per ottenere, se nessun'altra soluzione si è rivelata praticabile, una decisione esecutiva attraverso un meccanismo di arbitrato

MONITORAGGIO

Revisione annuale congiunta del funzionamento dell'Accordo

- Monitoraggio del funzionamento del *Privacy Shield* e del rispetto degli impegni assunti dagli USA anche con riguardo all'accesso ai dati per finalità di polizia e giustizia o di sicurezza nazionale
- La revisione sarà condotta dalla Commissione europea e dal *Department of Commerce* USA con il coinvolgimento di esperti dei servizi di sicurezza americani e delle Autorità europee per la protezione dei dati
- Previsto un vertice annuale, con la partecipazione di ONG e altri soggetti interessati, dedicato agli sviluppi nel settore della normativa privacy negli USA e al relativo impatto sugli europei
- La Commissione europea presenterà una relazione pubblica al Parlamento e al Consiglio, basandosi sui risultati della revisione annuale congiunta e su altre informazioni pertinenti (ad esempio, le relazioni sulla trasparenza presentate dalle imprese)

IN PRATICA

Le imprese americane

- Autocertificheranno su base annuale il rispetto degli obblighi
- Dovranno pubblicare una *privacy policy* (informativa privacy) sul loro sito
- Dovranno rispondere tempestivamente ai reclami
- Dovranno collaborare con le Autorità europee per la protezione dei dati e dare seguito alle loro richieste (se trattano dati relativi al personale/alle risorse umane)

Gli interessati in Europa

- Godranno di più trasparenza rispetto ai trasferimenti di dati personali negli USA e di una tutela rafforzata per questi dati
- Avranno a disposizione strumenti di tutela giuridica più facili da utilizzare e meno costosi in caso di reclami, che potranno gestire da soli oppure con l'aiuto dell'Autorità nazionale di protezione dei dati

FONTE: traduzione italiana di un *factsheet* della Commissione Europea DG Giustizia - anno 2016

Figure 9 - English translation of an infographic from the European Commission[233]

[233] Data Protection Authority, Privacy Shield, https://www.garanteprivacy.it/home/docweb/-/docweb-display/docweb/5306161 (permanent copy https://perma.cc/3HJG-YUGZ)

The draft "adequacy decision" then goes to the Article 29 Data *Protection Working* Party, the group for the protection of individuals with regard to the processing of personal data provided for in Article 29 of Directive 95/46/EC, in order to obtain an opinion and proceed with the final adoption of the decision.

On April 13, 2016, the group issues its opinion[234] stating that while there are greater safeguards than the *Safe Harbor*, three unresolved issues remain: U.S. organizations are not required to delete data when it is no longer needed, massive and indiscriminate collection of data by the U.S. administration is not completely ruled out, and the powers and position of the *Ombudsperson* require clarification to demonstrate its true independence and ability to intervene in the face of processing violations. On May 30, 2016, the *European Data Protection Supervisor* issued a[235] similar opinion: the *Privacy Shield*, as proposed, is not sufficiently robust to withstand scrutiny by the Court of Justice and believes significant improvements are needed before the European Commission adopts an adequacy decision.

On July 8, 2016, representatives of the EU member states, the committee provided for in Article 31 of Directive 95/46/EC, approve the final version of the Privacy Shield paving the way for the Commission to adopt the adequacy decision.

On July 12, 2016, the European Commission adopts Implementing Decision (EU) 2016/1250[236] *, pursuant to Directive 95/46/EC of the European Parliament and of the Council, on the adequacy of the protection offered by the EU-U.S. Privacy Shield regime.*

It is important to point out that "*The EU-U.S. Privacy Shield is based on a system of self-certification under which the U.S. organization commits to a set of privacy principles [...] with the specificity that a contract must bind the data controller to act solely in accordance with the instructions of the EU data controller and to assist it in responding to individuals exercising their rights under the* principles."[237] . The principles referred to are similar to those

---

[234] Article 29 Data Protection Working Party, Opinion 01/2016 on the EU - U.S. Privacy Shield draft adequacy decision,
https://ec.europa.eu/justice/article-29/documentation/opinion-recommendation/files/2016/wp238_en.pdf
(permanent copy *https://perma.cc/L96U-PLJU*)

[235] European Data Protection Supervisor, Privacy Shield: more robust and sustainable solution needed,
*https://secure.edps.europa.eu/EDPSWEB/webdav/site/mySite/shared/Documents/EDPS/PressNews/Press/2016/EDPS-2016-11-PrivacyShield_EN.*pdf
(permanent copy *https://perma.cc/FLL8-3K9H*)

[236] Commission Implementing Decision (EU) 2016/1250 of July 12, 2016, pursuant to Directive 95/46/EC of the European Parliament and of the Council, on the adequacy of the protection provided by the EU-U.S. Privacy Shield regime,
https://eur-lex.europa.eu/legal-content/IT/TXT/?uri=CELEX%3A32016D1250
(permanent copy https://perma.cc/8YLX-LC26)

[237] Implementing Decision (EU) 2016/1250, recital 14

also found in the previous *Safe Harbor* agreement: principle on disclosure[238] , principle on data integrity and purpose limitation[239] , principle on choice[240] , principle on security[241] , principle on access[242] , principle on redress, control and accountability[243] , principle on liability for further transfer[244] .

Regarding access and use by U.S. public authorities to the data transferred under the shield, the decision reports "the *Commission's analysis shows that the U.S. regulations provide a number of limitations [...] such that they constitute sufficient safeguards to effectively protect such data from unlawful interference and the risk of* abuse."[245] pointing out that as provided in Presidential Directive 68[246] "*the collection of intelligence data must always be 'as* targeted *as possible*'"[247] , "*certain circumstances sometimes oblige the services of the intelligence community to collect data in* bulk"[248] and "*in cases where bulk collection is unavoidable, the further use, through access, of the data so collected shall be strictly limited to precise legitimate* national *security purposes*"[249] . These considerations are also summarized in recital

---

238 Implementing Decision (EU) 2016/1250, recital 20, the organization is required to inform the data subject of a number of elements of fundamental importance to the processing of personal data concerning him or her (e.g., type of data collected, purpose of processing, right of access and choice, conditions applicable to further transfer, liability)

239 Implementing Decision (EU) 2016/1250, recitals 21 and 23, personal data collected must be limited to information that is relevant to the purpose of the processing, reliable for its intended use, accurate, complete, and up-to-date [...] personal information may only be kept in a form that identifies or allows for the identification of the data subject (i.e., in the form of personal data) for as long as necessary to achieve the purpose(s) for which it was originally collected or the purpose(s) subsequently authorized

240 Implementing Decision (EU) 2016/1250, recital 22, if the processing has a new (modified) purpose substantially different from the original purpose but still compatible with it, the principle on choice gives the data subject the right to refuse. [...] special rules apply to direct marketing that allow refusal "at any time" of the use of personal data [...] for sensitive data, the organization must normally obtain the explicit consent of the data subject (faculty of acceptance)

241 Implementing Decision (EU) 2016/1250, recital 24, the organization that creates, holds, uses or disseminates personal data must take "reasonable and appropriate" security measures, taking into account the risks inherent in the data processing and its nature

242 Implementing Decision (EU) 2016/1250, recital 25, the data subject shall have the right to know from the organization, without having to justify the request and for a non-excessive fee, whether it processes personal data concerning him or her and to obtain disclosure within a reasonable time [...] the data subject shall be able to correct, amend or delete personal information concerning him or her when it is inaccurate or when it has been processed in violation of the principles

243 Implementing Decision (EU) 2016/1250, Recital 26, the shield member organization must provide robust mechanisms to ensure compliance with the principles and redress for the EU data subject whose personal data has been processed in a non-compliant manner, including effective remedies

244 Implementing Decision (EU) 2016/1250, recitals 27, 28, and 29, further transfer is possible only for certain purposes, on the basis of a contract, providing the same level of protection guaranteed by the principles wherever the further recipient is located (in the United States or other third country)

245 Implementing Decision (EU) 2016/1250, recital 67.

246 Office of the Director of National Intelligence, Strengthening privacy & civil liberties protections, PPD-68, https://icontherecord.tumblr.com/ppd-28/2015/privacy-civil-liberties#ppd-28 (permanent copy https://perma.cc/Y5GY-TEHG)

247 Implementing Decision (EU) 2016/1250, recital 71

248 Implementing Decision (EU) 2016/1250, recital 72

249 Implementing Decision (EU) 2016/1250, recital 76

82, "*the U.S. government has also explicitly assured the Commission that the U.S. intelligence community 'does not conduct indiscriminate surveillance of anyone, and therefore not even the ordinary European citizen,'*" and in recital 90, "*the United States does not intend to conduct unlimited collection and storage of data about everyone without limitation, nor does it intend to allow unlimited access to the same [...] the signal intelligence activities conducted by the United States affect only a very small percentage of the communications that flow over the Internet.*"

The decision is implemented in our law by Order No. 436[250] of Oct. 27, 2016, in which the Data Protection Authority authorizes "*the transfer of data abroad through the agreement known as the EU-U.S. Privacy Shield.*"

Switzerland, following the path laid out by the European Union, will approve a similar agreement, *Swiss-U.S. Privacy Shield*, in January 2017: the agreement includes the same principles as the *EU-US Privacy Shield* with some distinctions such as, for example, the definition of "sensitive data" found in the choice principle[251] .

The CLOUD Act

As also predicted by Schrems himself in his evaluations following the Court of Justice of the European Union's October 2015 ruling, many U.S. companies, particularly large *hi-tech* companies, had been progressively relocating services to Europe over time, even before the final ruling, to ensure the proper processing of data even in the absence of a review of U.S. laws and international agreements. The purpose of the relocation of services is to demonstrate processing of personal data of European citizens without transfers to third countries.

The solution shows its potential effectiveness as early as 2013 when the *FBI*, requesting Microsoft for access to U.S. citizen emails stored on Irish *servers*, received a refusal. The rationale advanced by Microsoft is based on the fact that the *Stored Communications Act*[252] cannot compel U.S. companies to produce data stored in *servers* outside the United States of

---

[250] Garante per la Protezione dei Dati Personali, Provvedimento del 27 ottobre 2016, *https://www.garanteprivacy.it/home/docweb/-/docweb-display/docweb/5856335* (permanent copy https://perma.cc/SQX3-NWHT)

[251] White & Case, Swiss-U.S. Privacy Shield: Key Similarities, Key Distinctions with the EU-US Approach, *https://www.whitecase.com/publications/article/swiss-us-privacy-shield-key-similarities-key-distinctions-eu-us-approach* (permanent copy *https://perma.cc/U4TU-KM4N*)

[252] Wikipedia, Stored Communication Act, *https://en.wikipedia.org/wiki/Stored_Communications_Act* (permanent copy https://perma.cc/4WRV-45YR)

America. The case, known as *Microsoft Corp. v. United States*[253] , reaches the U.S. Supreme Court, which, in 2016, rules in favor of Microsoft. The U.S. Department of Justice then appeals.

While the case is still pending before the Supreme Court, Congress passes the *Clarifying Lawful Overseas Use of Data Act*[254] , known by its acronym *CLOUD Act*[255] , with the goal of updating the outdated language of the *Stored Communications Act* of 1986 and specifically including considerations on *cloud* storage for telecommunications companies regardless of *server* location. The act, included within a government spending bill, is enacted into law by President Donald Trump on March 23, 2018. The *CLOUD Act* requires *hi-tech* companies to provide stored data, of a customer or subscriber, on any *server* they own or operate when required by a warrant. The act allows companies to deny or challenge the request if the customer or subscriber is not a U.S. citizen and does not reside in the United States or if the provider believes it violates the privacy rights of the foreign country where the data is stored[256] . The *CLOUD Act* receives support from the U.S. Department of Justice and major corporations such as Microsoft, Apple, Google and Facebook[257] and is strongly criticized by several civil rights groups such as the Electronic Frontier Foundation and Amnesty International[258] because the rule would allow existing protections to be circumvented by making it significantly more difficult for governments in the countries where the *servers* are hosted to oversee them. This federal law, while not relevant to the events of the second Schrems ruling, highlights all the difficulties in succeeding in guaranteeing the right to privacy of European citizens' personal data in a reality dominated by globalized communications services operated primarily by U.S. companies.

---

[253] Wikipedia, Microsoft Corp. v. United States,
https://en.wikipedia.org/wiki/Microsoft_Corp._v._United_States
(permanent copy https://perma.cc/93RJ-SUNX)

[254] Congress of the United States of America, Clarifying Lawful Overseas Use of Data Act,
https://www.congress.gov/bill/115th-congress/senate-bill/2383/text
(permanent copy https://perma.cc/DM5E-TCBS)

[255] Wikipedia, CLOUD Act,
https://en.wikipedia.org/wiki/CLOUD_Act
(permanent copy https://perma.cc/SXN7-T4BS)

[256] Orrick Herrington & Sutcliffe, The CLOUD Act, Explained,
https://www.orrick.com/en/Insights/2018/04/The-CLOUD-Act-Explained
(permanent copy *https://perma.cc/J8JT-5494*)

[257] ZDNet, Microsoft bullish on Congress' inclusion of CLOUD Act in funding bill,
https://www.zdnet.com/article/microsoft-bullish-on-congress-inclusion-of-cloud-act-in-funding-bill/
(permanent copy *https://perma.cc/XRK5-R7HT*)

[258] The Verge, Vox Media, House passes controversial legislation giving the US more access to overseas data,
https://www.theverge.com/2018/3/22/17131004/cloud-act-congress-omnibus-passed-mlat
(permanent copy *https://perma.cc/A5TT-CD3E*)

The complaint

Before analyzing the events leading up to the second Schrems ruling, it is useful to give a brief summary of the events related to the first Schrems ruling. In 2013, Edward Snowden publicly revealed that U.S. *intelligence* agencies had access to the personal data of millions of people around the world based on the *PRISM* mass surveillance program. Major providers of electronic communication services, such as, for example, Apple, Facebook, Google, Microsoft, Yahoo and their subsidiaries, may be required to grant government authorities access to personal data of their users, including non-U.S. citizens or non-permanent residents of the United States.

After these revelations, Max Schrems, still a law student at the time, filed a complaint against Facebook Ireland Ltd. before the Irish data protection commissioner. The complaint alleges that under Decision 2000/520/EC, *EU-US Safe Harbor*, a European citizen's data cannot be sent from Facebook Ireland Ltd. provider for users outside the U.S. and Canada to Facebook Inc. headquartered in the U.S., since the latter must grant government agencies access to such data. The Irish commissioner rejects the complaint, calling the charge "frivolous and vexatious" and arguing that the European Commission has already made its adequacy assessment by adopting Decision 2000/520/EC. Schrems then applies to the *Irish High Court for* review, which refers the case to the Court of Justice of the European Union for a reassessment of the *Safe Harbor* Decision. In October 2015, the Court of Justice of the European Union issues its ruling: a third country such as the United States must provide a level of protection substantially equivalent to European Union law and legislation that allows government authorities to have access on a blanket basis violates the essence of fundamental rights to privacy under Article 7 of the Charter of Fundamental Rights of the European Union therefore Decision 2000/520/EC is declared invalid.

It was only following the ruling of the Court of Justice of the European Union that he informed Schrems that the ruling on the *Safe Harbor* decision was irrelevant to the assessment of the complaint filed in 2013 because the data transfer made by Facebook was based on the standard contractual clauses, *standard contractual clauses*, also known by the acronym *SCCs.*

On December 1, 2015, Schrems resubmitted his complaint against Facebook to the Irish commissioner by including the standard contractual clauses that Facebook relies on. The clauses[259] of the contract between Facebook Ireland Ltd. and Facebook Inc. differ significantly from those in the annex to Decision 2010/87/EU[260] *on standard contractual clauses for the transfer of personal data to processors established in third countries under Directive 95/46/EC of the European Parliament and of the Council*, in particular, clause 2 gives priority to other intra-group agreements within Facebook, second paragraph, and to other obscured and unspecified agreements, third paragraph.

The two images below show the profound differences between the text provided in the annex to Decision 2010/87/EU and what is in the contract between Facebook Ireland Ltd. and Facebook Inc.

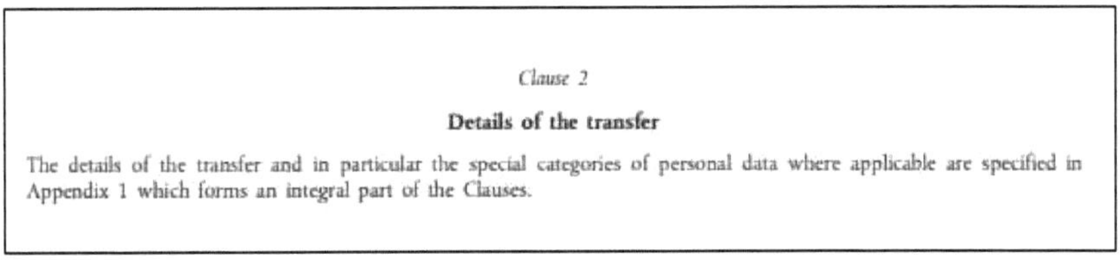

Clause 2

Details of the transfer

The details of the transfer and in particular the special categories of personal data where applicable are specified in Appendix 1 which forms an integral part of the Clauses.

Figure 10 - Clause 2 of the Annex to Decision 2010/87/EU.[261]

[259] Europe v. Facebook, Facebook Ireland's data sharing deal with Facebook USA of Nov 2015, *http://www.europe-v-facebook.org/comp_fb_scc.pdf* (permanent copy https://perma.cc/HJ3P-5CKQ)

[260] Commission Decision 2010/87/EU of February 5, 2010 , on standard contractual clauses for the transfer of personal data to processors established in third countries under Directive 95/46/EC of the European Parliament and of the Council, *https://eur-lex.europa.eu/legal-content/IT/TXT/?uri=CELEX%3A32010D0087* (permanent copy https://perma.cc/3NWA-4426)

[261] Commission Decision 2010/87/EU, of February 5, 2010, on standard contractual clauses for the transfer of personal data to processors established in third countries under Directive 95/46/EC of the European Parliament and of the Council, Annex, page 7, *https://eur-lex.europa.eu/legal-content/EN/TXT/PDF/?uri=CELEX:32010D0087&from=IT* (permanent copy *https://perma.cc/ZA5S-UPAS*)

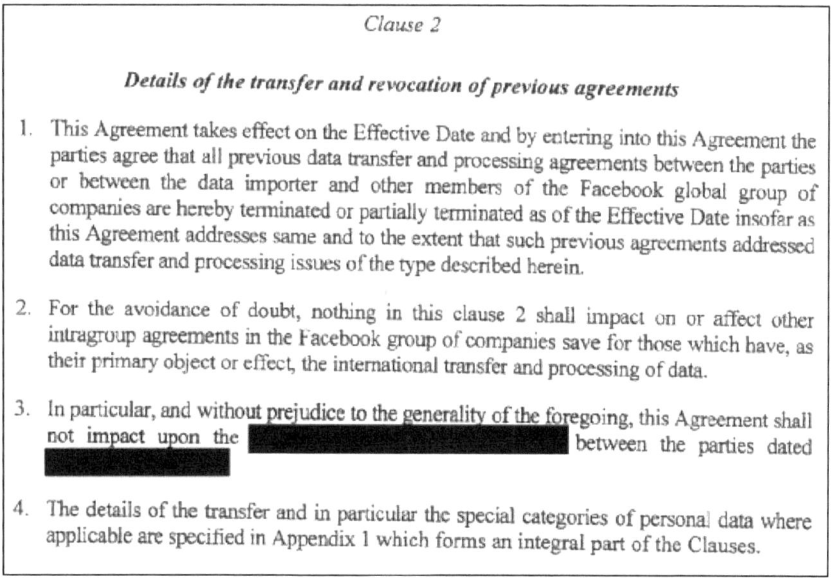

Clause 2

Details of the transfer and revocation of previous agreements

1. This Agreement takes effect on the Effective Date and by entering into this Agreement the parties agree that all previous data transfer and processing agreements between the parties or between the data importer and other members of the Facebook global group of companies are hereby terminated or partially terminated as of the Effective Date insofar as this Agreement addresses same and to the extent that such previous agreements addressed data transfer and processing issues of the type described herein.

2. For the avoidance of doubt, nothing in this clause 2 shall impact on or affect other intragroup agreements in the Facebook group of companies save for those which have, as their primary object or effect, the international transfer and processing of data.

3. In particular, and without prejudice to the generality of the foregoing, this Agreement shall not impact upon the [redacted] between the parties dated [redacted]

4. The details of the transfer and in particular the special categories of personal data where applicable are specified in Appendix 1 which forms an integral part of the Clauses.

Figure 11 - Clause 2 of the contract between Facebook Ireland Ltd. and Facebook Inc.[262]

Schrems' argument can be summarized by Article 1 of the Decision: only "*the standard contractual clauses set out in the Annex constitute sufficient safeguards for the protection of the privacy and fundamental rights and freedoms of individuals and for the exercise of related rights under Article 26(2) of Directive 95/46/EC.*" The request made by Schrems is to suspend all data transfers from Facebook Ireland Ltd. to Facebook Inc. with a reasonable implementation period that allows Facebook Ireland Ltd. to undertake all necessary technical and organizational steps, e.g., processing of personal data within the European Economic Area or any third country, other than the United States of America, that provides adequate protection guarantees.

The Irish commissioner asks the *Irish High Court* to issue a new referral to the Court of Justice of the European Union holding that the standard contractual clauses do not provide a legal mechanism for the transfer of data if a third country, such as the United States of America, provides conflicting laws. After several procedural steps including the participation

[262] Europe v. Facebook, Facebook Ireland's data sharing deal with Facebook USA of Nov 2015, page 3, http://www.europe-v-facebook.org/comp_fb_scc.pdf (permanent copy https://perma.cc/HJ3P-5CKQ)

of numerous experts on U.S. surveillance law, the IEHC 545[263] ruling on October 3, 2017 recognized the existence of mass surveillance programs by the U.S. government[264] and, on April 13, 2018, the *Irish High Court* referred eleven interpretive questions to the Court of Justice of the European Union[265] . Among the most significant questions[266] are the examination of the possible violation of rights under Articles 7 and 8 of the Charter of Fundamental Rights of the European Union in relation to the processing of data by the U.S. government for national security purposes[267] , the analysis of the guarantees offered by the standard contractual clauses in relation to the transfer to an importer who is obligated by national authorities to share the processed data[268] , and the assessment of the Enforcement Decision (EU) 2016/1250, *Privacy Shield EU-US*, as a sufficient guarantee of an adequate level of protection[269] . Interestingly, the *Irish High Court*'s request anticipates the implementation date of the new Regulation (EU) 2016/679 by a few days so Directive 95/46/EC is the standard of reference in many of the questions addressed to the Court of Justice of the European Union.

---

263 Irish High Court, Judgment of Ms. Justice Costello delivered on the 3rd day of October, 2017, *https://www.courts.ie/viewer/pdf/20863258-a092-4111-95fd-deefd38e6fd9/2017_IEHC_545_1.pdf/pdf#view=fitH* (permanent copy *https://perma.cc/2JE4-3X2E*)

264 TechCrunch, Privacy Shield now facing questions via legal challenge to Facebook data flows, *https://techcrunch.com/2018/04/13/privacy-shield-now-facing-questions-via-legal-challenge-to-facebook-data-flows/* (permanent copy https://perma.cc/F4Z2-BVGU)

265 Alston & Bird, Irish High Court Refers Schrems 2.0 to the ECJ, *https://www.alstonprivacy.com/irish-high-court-refers-schrems-2-0-to-the-ecj/* (permanent copy *https://perma.cc/J83S-VZLW*)

266 Case C-311/18: Reference for a preliminary ruling brought by the High Court (Ireland) on May 9, 2018, Data Protection Commissioner v. Facebook Ireland Limited, Maximilian Schrems, *https://eur-lex.europa.eu/legal-content/IT/TXT/?uri=CELEX%3A62018CN0311* (permanent copy https://perma.cc/2NA8-B3G8)

267 Question 4, Given the facts found by the High Court in relation to US law, if personal data is transferred from the EU to the US under the SCC Decision does this violate the rights of individuals under Articles 7 and/or 8 of the Charter?

268 Question 7, Does the fact that the standard contractual clauses apply as between the data exporter and the data importer and do not bind the national authorities of a third country who may require the data importer to make available to its security services for further processing the personal data transferred pursuant to the clauses provided for in the SCC Decision preclude the clauses from adducing adequate safeguards as envisaged by Article 26(2) of the Directive?

269 Question 9, For the purposes of Article 25(6) of the Directive, does Decision (EU) 2016/1250 ('the Privacy Shield Decision') constitute a finding of general application binding on data protection authorities and the courts of the member states to the effect that the US ensures an adequate level of protection within the meaning of Article 25(2) of the Directive by reason of its domestic law or of the international commitments it has entered into?

The judgment

The case in the Court of Justice of the European Union is C-311/18[270] : the plaintiff is the European Commissioner while the respondents are Facebook Ireland Ltd. and Maximilian Schrems.

The case also involves the U.S. government, the Electronic Privacy Information Centre foundation[271] and the two *lobbies* Business Software Alliance[272] and Digitaleurope[273] as representatives of more than one hundred U.S. and European *hi-tech* companies including Amazon, Apple, Cisco, Facebook, Google, Intel, Microsoft, Nokia, Oracle and Samsung.

The advocate general of the court is Henrik Saugmandsgaard Øe[274] who rejects the objection made by Facebook Ireland Ltd. regarding the admissibility of the reference for a preliminary ruling on the basis of the repeal of Directive 95/46/EC, to which the questions refer[275] . The Advocate General's analysis considers both pieces of reference legislation, Directive 95/46/EC and Regulation (EU) 2016/679, but also Decision 2010/87/EU *on standard contractual clauses for the transfer of personal data to processors established in third countries under Directive 95/46/EC of the European Parliament and of the Council*, and Implementing Decision (EU) 2016/1250, *Privacy Shield EU-US.*

In his analysis, the Advocate General sets out similarities and differences with the *PNR* judgment[276] , *Passenger Name Records*: "*In the PNR judgment, the court annulled the*

---

[270] Court of Justice of the European Union, case number C-311/18, *https://curia.europa.eu/juris/documents.jsf?oqp=&for=&mat=or&lgrec=de&jge=&td=%3BALL&jur=C%2CT%2CF&num=C-311%252F18&page=1&dates=&pcs=Oor&lg=&pro=&nat=or&cit=none%252*CC%252CCJ%252CR%252C2008E%252C%252C%252C%252C%252C%252C%252C%252C%252C%252Ctrue%252Cfalse%252Cfalse&language=en&avg=&cid=6150195 (permanent copy https://perma.cc/ZAS4-LPX5)

[271] Electronic Privacy Information Center, *https://epic.org/about/* (permanent copy https://perma.cc/SK5F-2WJV)

[272] BSA, The Software Alliance, *https://www.bsa.org/about-bsa* (permanent copy https://perma.cc/H733-DM3S)

[273] DigitalEurope, *https://www.digitaleurope.org/about-us/* (permanent copy https://perma.cc/9WWR-5FN7)

[274] Wikipedia, Henrik Saugmandsgaard Øe, *https://da.wikipedia.org/wiki/Henrik_Saugmandsgaard_%C3%98e* (permanent copy https://perma.cc/C84Y-WHEF)

[275] Opinion of Advocate General Henrik Saugmandsgaard Øe delivered December 19, 2019, Case C-311/18, paragraphs 88 to 93, *https://eur-lex.europa.eu/legal-content/it/TXT/?uri=CELEX:62018CC0311* (permanent copy https://perma.cc/A2B9-C5KH)

[276] Court of Justice of the European Union, Judgment of the Court (Grand Chamber), May 30, 2006, Joined Cases C-317/04, Protection of Individuals with Regard to the Processing of Personal Data - Air Transport,

decision in which the Commission had found the adequacy of the level of protection of personal data contained in the Passenger Name Records (PNR) of air passengers transferred to the U.S. Customs and Border Protection authority[277] ". On that occasion, the court had ruled that the transfer fell within the exclusionary scope of Directive 95/46/EC: although *PNR* data were initially collected by private operators in the context of a commercial activity, such processing was necessary within a framework established by public authorities to ensure the safeguarding of public security. In this case it is necessary to consider two fundamental aspects with respect to the processing of personal data transferred by Facebook to the United States of America and subsequently acquired by *intelligence* agencies: the guarantee of predictability and proportionality of U.S. governmental interference for national security[278] and the effective availability of enforceable rights and effective remedies by data subjects[279] .

The selection criteria used to collect the information are not sufficiently clear and precise to provide sufficient guarantees to prevent the risk of abuse. The criteria themselves are not individually approved by an independent judicial or administrative body prior to their application, and furthermore, no prior assessment is taken that, based on the plausible elements, would allow for a determination of whether the person subject to interception is truly a suitable target for acquiring external *intelligence* information. The safeguards offered by Enforcement Decision (EU) 2016/1250, *Privacy Shield EU-US,* are therefore not deemed "*sufficient to meet the conditions of 'predictability' and 'necessity in a democratic society*'."

The Fourth Amendment[280] of the U.S. Constitution, which would be the most important protection against unlawful surveillance, does not appear to apply to EU-US citizens who do not have a voluntary and meaningful connection to the United States[281] , *Executive Order*

---

and C-318/04, Agreement between the European Community and the United States of America - Air Passenger Name Records Transferred to the U.S. Bureau of Customs and Border Protection, *https://curia.europa.eu/juris/document/document.jsf?text=&docid=56830&pageIndex=0&doclang=IT&* mode=req&dir=&occ=first&part=1&cid=1198707 (permanent copy https://perma.cc/3MWN-5NS8)

277 Opinion of Advocate General Henrik Saugmandsgaard Øe delivered December 19, 2019, Case C-311/18, paragraphs 213 to 220, *https://eur-lex.europa.eu/legal-content/it/TXT/?uri=CELEX:62018CC0311* (permanent copy https://perma.cc/A2B9-C5KH)

278 GDPR, Article 23 - Limitations, paragraph 1, *https://gdpr-text.com/it/read/article-23/#para_gdpr-a-23_1* (permanent copy https://perma.cc/F97P-LKJR)

279 GDPR, Article 46 - Transfer subject to adequate safeguards, para, *https://gdpr-text.com/it/read/article-46/#para_gdpr-a-46_1* (permanent copy https://perma.cc/PG9D-JLGN)

280 Fourth Amendment of the Constitution of the United States of America, *https://constitution.congress.gov/constitution/amendment-4/* (permanent copy https://perma.cc/6YGT-N3GP)

281 Conclusions of Advocate General Henrik Saugmandsgaard Øe delivered December 19, 2019, Case C-311/18,

12333 and PPD-28 "*expressly mention that they do not confer legally enforceable rights on data subjects*[282] *[...] are rather akin to internal administrative instructions, which may be revoked or modified by the president of the* United *States.*"[283] and the Ombudsman introduced by the *EU-US Privacy Shield* is appointed by the Secretary of State and is an integral part of the U.S. Department of State therefore it is not an independent body from the executive power[284] . Data subjects therefore have no enforceable rights and no effective remedies.

On December 19, 2019, the Advocate General delivers his conclusions[285] : does not find "*elements capable of affecting the validity of Commission Decision 2010/87/EU of February 5, 2010 on standard contractual clauses for the transfer of personal data to processors established in third countries under Directive 95/46/EC of the European Parliament and of the Council, as amended by Commission Implementing Decision (EU) 2016/2297 of December 16, 2016,*" and highlights the need to reassess the "*compliance of the Privacy Shield Decision with Article 45(1) of the [GDPR], read in light of Articles 7, 8 and 47 of the Charter and Article 8* ECHR."[286] . The existence of such an adequacy decision prevents a national supervisory authority, in this case the Irish commissioner, from suspending or prohibiting the transfer of data to the United States.

---

para. 66,
https://eur-lex.europa.eu/legal-content/it/TXT/?uri=CELEX:62018CC0311
(permanent copy https://perma.cc/A2B9-C5KH)

282 Executive Order 12333, Section 3.7 - General Provisions, paragraph (c), this order is intended only to improve the internal management of the executive branch and is not intended to, and does not, create any right or benefit, substantive or procedural, enforceable at law or in equity, by any party against the United States, its departments, agencies or entities, its officers, employees, or agents, or any other person,
https://irp.fas.org/offdocs/eo/eo-13470.htm
(permanent copy https://perma.cc/Y6HF-XB7B)

283 Conclusions of Advocate General Henrik Saugmandsgaard Øe delivered December 19, 2019, Case C-311/18, para. 267,
https://eur-lex.europa.eu/legal-content/it/TXT/?uri=CELEX:62018CC0311
(permanent copy https://perma.cc/A2B9-C5KH)

284 Conclusions of Advocate General Henrik Saugmandsgaard Øe delivered December 19, 2019, Case C-311/18, para. 337,
https://eur-lex.europa.eu/legal-content/it/TXT/?uri=CELEX:62018CC0311
(permanent copy https://perma.cc/A2B9-C5KH)

285 Court of Justice of the European Union, Opinion of Advocate General Henrik Saugmandsgaard Øe delivered December 19, 2019, Case C-311/18,
https://curia.europa.eu/juris/document/document.jsf?text=&docid=221826&pageIndex=0&doclang=IT& mode=req&dir=&occ=first&part=1&cid=7324556
(permanent copy https://perma.cc/62AV-XS52)

286 Conclusions of Advocate General Henrik Saugmandsgaard Øe delivered December 19, 2019, Case C-311/18, para. 342,
https://eur-lex.europa.eu/legal-content/it/TXT/?uri=CELEX:62018CC0311
(permanent copy https://perma.cc/A2B9-C5KH)

The court issues its ruling[287] on July 16, 2020 responding to the eleven issues raised by the *Irish High Court.*

In relation to the first question[288] , the court finds that it falls within the scope of Regulation (EU) 2016/679 "*a transfer of personal data carried out for commercial purposes by an economic operator established in a member state to another economic operator established in a third country, notwithstanding the fact that, during or following such a transfer, the said data may be subject to processing by the authorities of the third country in question for the purposes of public security, defense and* state *security.*"[289] .

In relation to the second[290] , third[291] and sixth[292] question, the court specifies that "*the adequate safeguards, enforceable rights and effective remedies required by these provisions must ensure that the rights of individuals whose personal data are transferred to a third country on the basis of standard data protection clauses enjoy a level of protection that is substantially equivalent to that guaranteed within the* Union."[293] .

In relation to the eighth question[294] , the court states that, "*unless there is an adequacy decision validly adopted by the Commission, the competent supervisory authority is obliged to*

---

[287] Court of Justice of the European Union, Judgment of the Court (Grand Chamber) July 16, 2020, Case C-311/18,
https://curia.europa.eu/juris/document/document.jsf?text=&docid=228677&pageIndex=0&doclang=IT&
mode=req&dir=&occ=first&part=1&cid=7324556
(permanent copy https://perma.cc/5S7Q-JGHC)

[288] Does EU law apply in the case of personal data transferred for commercial purposes from a private company in an EU member state to a private company in a third country and then further processed for national security purposes by third country authorities

[289] Judgment of the Court (Grand Chamber) of July 16, 2020, Case C-311/18, paragraph 89,
https://eur-lex.europa.eu/legal-content/IT/TXT/HTML/?uri=CELEX:62018CJ0311&from=it
(permanent copy https://perma.cc/23Y3-UZSC)

[290] Whether, in determining a violation of an individual's rights due to the transfer of data from the Union to a third country where it may be further processed for national security purposes, the touchstone is the Charter of Fundamental Rights of the European Union, the Treaty of the European Union (the so-called "Maastricht Treaty"), the Treaty on the Functioning of the European Union (the so-called "Lisbon Treaty"), the Directive (the "Regulation") and any other provision of Union law or the national laws of one or more member states

[291] Whether, in determining a violation of an individual's rights due to the transfer of data from the Union to a third country in which it may be further processed for national security purposes, only the national legislation and international commitments of the third country should be assessed or also the practices, safeguards, procedures, means of control and remedies in place

[292] What is the required level of protection that must be afforded to personal data transferred to a third country under the standard contractual clauses, and what are the factors to be considered in assessing whether the level of protection afforded to data transferred to a third country meets the requirements of the Directive and the Charter of Fundamental Rights of the European Union

[293] Judgment of the Court (Grand Chamber) of July 16, 2020, Case C-311/18, paragraph 105,
https://eur-lex.europa.eu/legal-content/IT/TXT/HTML/?uri=CELEX:62018CJ0311&from=it
(permanent copy https://perma.cc/23Y3-UZSC)

[294] Where importer of data from a third country is subject to surveillance rules that, in the opinion of a data protection authority, are contrary to the clauses of the Annex to the CCT Decision or Articles 25 and 26 of the Directive and/or the Charter, is a data protection authority required to use its enforcement powers in order to suspend data flows or is the exercise of such powers limited only to exceptional cases

suspend or prohibit a transfer of data to a third country made on the basis of standard data protection clauses adopted by the Commission, if that supervisory authority considers, in light of the totality of the circumstances peculiar to that transfer, that the said clauses are not or cannot be complied with in that third *country."*[295] .

In relation to the seventh[296] and eleventh[297] question, the court finds that the examination of Decision 2010/87/EU, in light of Articles 7, 8 and 47 of the Charter of Fundamental Rights of the European Union, has not revealed anything that would affect its validity[298] .

In relation to the fourth[299] , fifth[300] , ninth[301] and tenth[302] issues, the court concludes that "*the Privacy Shield Decision is invalid*: is binding on the supervisory authorities insofar as it finds that the United States guarantees an adequate level of protection therefore it has the effect of authorizing transfers of personal data by preventing their suspension or prohibition by the supervisory authorities[303] , the Ombudsman is not assimilated to a judge within the meaning of Article 47 of the Charter of Fundamental Rights of the European Union[304] , *PPD-28 does* not confer on data subjects actionable rights against the U.S. authorities before the courts therefore the decision is not suitable to guarantee a substantially equivalent level of

---

295 Judgment of the Court (Grand Chamber) July 16, 2020, Case C-311/18, paragraph 121, *https://eur-lex.europa.eu/legal-content/IT/TXT/HTML/?uri=CELEX:62018CJ0311&from=it* (permanent copy https://perma.cc/23Y3-UZSC)

296 Does the fact that the standard contractual clauses between the data exporter and the data importer do not bind the national authorities of a third country, which may require the data importer to make the data transferred from the Union available to the security services, preclude the clauses from offering sufficient guarantees

297 Whether the decision on standard contract clauses violates Articles 7, 8 and/or 47 of the Charter

298 Judgment of the Court (Grand Chamber) July 16, 2020, Case C-311/18, paragraph 149, *https://eur-lex.europa.eu/legal-content/IT/TXT/HTML/?uri=CELEX:62018CJ0311&from=it* (permanent copy https://perma.cc/23Y3-UZSC)

299 Whether, considering the facts established by the Irish High Court, the transfer of personal data from the Union to the United States violates the rights of individuals under Articles 7 and 8 of the Charter of Fundamental Rights of the European Union

300 Whether, considering the facts established by the Irish High Court, in the case of the transfer of personal data from the European Union to the United States pursuant to the decision on standard contractual clauses, the level of protection afforded by the United States respects an individual's essential right to a judicial remedy in the event of a violation of his or her data protection rights

301 Does Decision (EU) 2016/1250, EU-US Privacy Shield, constitute a finding of general application that binds the data protection authorities and courts of the Member States, in the sense that the United States ensures an adequate level of protection by reason of its domestic legislation or international commitments it has entered into

302 Given the findings of the Irish High Court, does the establishment of the Ombudsman under Decision (EU) 2016/1250, Privacy Shield, in conjunction with the regime in place in the United States, guarantee a means of redress in favor of data subjects

303 Judgment of the Court (Grand Chamber) July 16, 2020, Case C-311/18, paragraph 156, *https://eur-lex.europa.eu/legal-content/IT/TXT/HTML/?uri=CELEX:62018CJ0311&from=it* (permanent copy https://perma.cc/23Y3-UZSC)

304 Judgment of the Court (Grand Chamber) July 16, 2020, Case C-311/18, paragraph 168, *https://eur-lex.europa.eu/legal-content/IT/TXT/HTML/?uri=CELEX:62018CJ0311&from=it* (permanent copy https://perma.cc/23Y3-UZSC)

protection[305] . The court notes that the annulment of the adequacy decision is not likely to create a legal loophole, in fact, Article 49 of the *GDPR* sets out precisely under what conditions transfers of personal data to third countries can take place in the absence of an adequacy decision under Article 45 or appropriate safeguards under Article 46 of the regulation.

The ruling of the Court of Justice of the European Union, which will remain known as the "Schrems II Judgment," thus confirms the validity of standard contractual clauses for the transfer of personal data to data controllers outside the European Economic Area while invalidating the *EU-US Privacy Shield. A* few days later, on September 8, 2020, the *Swiss Federal Data Protection and Information Commissioner ("SDPIC")* will invalidate the similar existing agreement between Switzerland and the United States of America, *Swiss-U.S. Privacy Shield Framework*[306] .

Evaluations

Initial reactions to the ruling of the Court of Justice of the European Union can, of course, be found on the *NOYB* website[307] . Max Schrems, the organization's president and a party to the case, believes that the ruling represents a blow to the Irish commissioner, to Facebook, but also, and most importantly, to the United States of America, which will necessarily have to enact a radical reform of its surveillance laws to enable overseas companies to remain competitive in the EU market. Harsh, too, was his assessment of the European Commission, which in 2016 had adopted Implementing Decision (EU) 2016/1250 without a thorough and accurate assessment of the surveillance laws in place in the United States of America.

The comment by Herwig Hofmann, professor of law at the University of Luxembourg and one of the advocates in the Schrems cases before the Court of Justice of the European Union, is particularly telling: "*The court invalidated the Commission's second decision, which violates the European Union's fundamental rights to data protection. There can be no transfer*

[305] Judgment of the Court (Grand Chamber) of July 16, 2020, Case C-311/18, paragraph 181, *https://eur-lex.europa.eu/legal-content/IT/TXT/HTML/?uri=CELEX:62018CJ0311&from=it* (permanent copy https://perma.cc/23Y3-UZSC)

[306] Privacy Shield Framework, FAQs - Swiss-U.S. Privacy Shield, *https://www.privacyshield.gov/article?id=Swiss-U-S-Privacy-Shield-FAQs* (permanent copy *https://perma.cc/6PZB-69F7*)

[307] NOYB, CJEU Judgment - First Statemens, CJEU invalidates "Privacy Shield" in US Surveillance case. SCCs cannot be used by Facebook and similar companies, *https://noyb.eu/en/cjeu* (permanent copy https://perma.cc/ZP7B-MCFR)

of data to a country with forms of mass surveillance. As long as U.S. law gives its government the power to acquire European data in transit to the United States, such instruments will always be doomed to annulment."[308] . The lawyer's words thus seem to anticipate the outcome of the probable new adequacy decision presented by the European Commission in late March 2022, referred to by many as *Privacy Shield 2.0*: independent of international agreements signed between the European Union and the United States of America or self-certifications made by U.S. companies, it will not be possible to guarantee data protection rights, enforceable rights and effective remedies for European citizens unless U.S. law is thoroughly overhauled.

As Schrems' words anticipated, the ruling is not limited to the single case of Facebook Ireland Ltd. and Facebook Inc. but has a profound impact on all U.S. *hi-tech* companies: on July 24, 2022, the *NOYB* organization, is promoting an awareness campaign[309] and invites users of Amazon, Apple, Google, Facebook, Instagram, Microsoft, Twitter, Yahoo and any other public or private organization to send an email to the other party requesting whether their personal data are being transferred to third countries and which ones, whether the transfer is authorized by an adequacy decision, standard contractual clauses, binding corporate rules or other exemptions, whether the data is subject to further transfer to the U.S. government, what technical measures are being applied to prevent the possible interception of data in transit, and highlighting the willingness to immediately stop the data transfer. In the absence of a response from the service provider, *NOYB* suggests sending a complaint to the local supervisory authority citing the C311/18 - Schrems II ruling and requesting investigation into the matter to order the suspension or prohibition of the processing. At the end of September 2020, the *NOYB* organization publishes an account[310] of the responses received from network users: the list[311] includes more than thirty companies including, in addition to those already mentioned above, Airbnb, American Express, Booking, Ebay, LinkedIn, Mastercard, Netflix,

---

308 The CJEU has invalidated the second Commission decision violating EU fundamental data protection rights. There can be no transfer of data to a country with forms of mass surveillance. As long as US law gives its government the powers to vacuum-up EU data transiting to the US, such instruments will be invalidated again and again

309 NOYB, Next Steps for users & FAQs, https://noyb.eu/en/next-steps-users-faqs (permanent copy https://perma.cc/CW6B-HEPT)

310 NOYB, Companies can't say how they comply with CJEU ruling, https://noyb.eu/en/companies-cant-say-how-they-comply-cjeu-ruling (permanent copy https://perma.cc/HD7V-QAMU)

311 NOYB, Opening Pandora's Box: How companies addressed our questions about their international data transfers after the CJEU's ruling in C-311/18 - Schrems II, https://noyb.eu/sites/default/files/2021-10/Replies_from_controllers_on_EU-US_transfers.pdf (permanent copy https://perma.cc/WJB9-JZKZ)

Tinder, Zoom. In many cases, the companies did not respond to the request for information or redirected the user to the *privacy policy* page on the website where, however, there are no detailed explanations. Only an extremely small group of companies, including Microsoft and Virgin Media, responded fully and sent a copy of the model contract clauses. Plausibly none of the companies contacted have suspended the transfer of data from the European Union to the United States of America.

The ruling, while recognizing the validity of the standard contractual clauses, indirectly highlights the need for their revision in light of the repeal of Directive 95/46/EC in favor of the new Regulation (EU) 2016/679, e.g., Decision 2010/87/EE on standard contractual clauses, while referring to the directive, does not contain any reference to the data controller, who is responsible for determining the purposes and means of the processing of personal data, and the controller, who is in charge of processing personal data on behalf of the data controller. The changes introduced do not stop there: standard contractual clauses alone cannot guarantee an equivalent level of protection in the case of transfers to third countries where the importer is subject to interference by government authorities so they must be supplemented with appropriate technical measures, such as encryption and pseudonymization. The content of the decision on new standard contractual clauses will be analyzed in more detail in 0.

Chapter 4.
The new standard contract clauses

The recent model contractual clauses[312] see the light of day more than a decade after the adoption of the previous text[313] in a context that has been characterized over time by the Schrems I judgment and the subsequent declaration of invalidity of *Safe Harbor*, the repeal of Directive 95/46/EC and the subsequent entry into force of the new Regulation (EU) 2016/679, and, as the last act, the Schrems II judgment and the subsequent declaration of invalidity of the *Privacy Shield.* The ruling, while also confirming the validity of the standard contractual clauses for the transfer of personal data to third countries for which an adequacy decision is not available, highlighted the need for a new version of the standard contractual clauses to align their text with the new regulation and provide technical tools and practical solutions to bring processing into compliance with the court's decision.

The Implementing Decision (EU) 2021/914 of June 4, 2021

On June 4, 2021, the European Commission adopts two sets of standard contractual clauses[314] , one for use between data controllers and processors and one for the transfer of personal data to third countries. The two texts reflect new requirements under Regulation (EU) 2016/679 and take into account the Court of Justice of the European Union's Schrems II ruling to ensure a high level of data protection for citizens. The aim of the new standard contractual clauses is to allow the free movement of data, including to third countries, provided that their protection is guaranteed during each transfer[315] .

---

312 Commission Implementing Decision (EU) 2021/914 of June 4, 2021, on standard contractual clauses for the transfer of personal data to third countries under Regulation (EU) 2016/679 of the European Parliament and of the Council,
https://eur-lex.europa.eu/legal-content/IT/TXT/HTML/?uri=CELEX:32021D0914
(permanent copy https://perma.cc/T986-DUY8)

313 Commission Decision 2010/87/EU of 5 February 2010 on standard contractual clauses for the transfer of personal data to processors established in third countries under Directive 95/46/EC of the European Parliament and of the Council

314 European Commission, European Commission adopts new tools for safe exchanges of personal data,
https://ec.europa.eu/commission/presscorner/detail/it/ip_21_2847
(permanent copy https://perma.cc/5U86-AJ8Z)

315 Vera Jourová, Vice-President for Values and Transparency: "In Europe, we want to remain open and allow data to flow, provided that the protection flows with it. The modernised Standard Contractual Clauses will help to achieve this objective: they offer businesses a useful tool to ensure they comply with data protection laws, both for their activities within the EU and for international transfers. This is a needed solution in the interconnected digital world where transferring data takes a click or two."

The new standard contract clauses provide an approved template that companies can implement with the final assurance that the contract meets data protection requirements. Key new features include an update in line with the new Regulation (EU) 2016/679, a modular structure to accommodate even complex transfer chains, and a practical approach based on technical advice and additional measures that companies can take.

The text, consisting of twenty-six recitals, four articles, and an annex with the structure of standard contractual clauses, refers several times to the Schrems II judgment: recital 1 recalls "*the provisions on data transfers in Chapter V of Regulation (EU) 2016/679 intended to ensure the continuity of the high level of protection when personal data are transferred to a third country*," recital 11 highlights the importance of standard contractual clauses capable of "*ensuring that personal data transferred on their basis are afforded a level of protection substantially equivalent to that afforded within the Union.*" recital 18 emphasizes the need for "*specific safeguards, particularly in light of the case law of the Court of Justice, to address any effects of the law of the third country of destination on the importer's compliance with the clauses, particularly with regard to how to deal with binding requests from public authorities in the third country to disclose transferred personal data.*"

Article 1[316] identifies the contractual clauses set out in the Annex as "*appropriate safeguards within the meaning of Articles 46(1) and 46(2)(c) of Regulation (EU) 2016/679 for the purposes of the transfer from a controller or processor of personal data processed subject to that Regulation (exporter) to a controller or (sub)controller whose data processing is not subject to that Regulation (importer).*" Article 2[317] recalls the possibility for the competent authorities of the member states to suspend or prohibit the transfer, informing the Commission and other states, "*where the importer is or has become subject to legislation or practice in the third country of destination that prevents him from complying with the standard contractual clauses.*" Article 3[318] establishes a periodic reassessment mechanism by the Commission similar to that provided for in

---

[316] Commission Implementing Decision (EU) 2021/914 of June 4, 2021 on standard contractual clauses for the transfer of personal data to third countries under Regulation (EU) 2016/679 of the European Parliament and of the Council, Article 1, *https://eur-lex.europa.eu/legal-content/IT/TXT/HTML/?uri=CELEX:32021D0914&from=EN#d1e335-31-1* (permanent copy https://perma.cc/26N4-MEGC)

[317] Commission Implementing Decision (EU) 2021/914, Article 2, *https://eur-lex.europa.eu/legal-content/IT/TXT/HTML/?uri=CELEX:32021D0914&from=EN#d1e348-31-1* (permanent copy https://perma.cc/R5BN-VJAZ)

[318] Commission Implementing Decision (EU) 2021/914, Article 3, *https://eur-lex.europa.eu/legal-content/IT/TXT/HTML/?uri=CELEX:32021D0914&from=EN#d1e353-31-1* (permanent copy https://perma.cc/H4VM-BXWY)

Article 97 of Regulation (EU) 2016/679, and Article 4[319] sets out the repeal of the previous decision and transitional rules for existing contracts.

The model contract clauses and annexes

There are eighteen standard contractual clauses designed to ensure compliance with the requirements of Regulation (EU) 2016/679 when transferring personal data to a third country, organized into four sections.

The first section contains the general provisions. Clause 1, *purpose and scope*, gives the definitions of exporter, importer, purpose and scope of the contract which will be detailed in Annex 1. The role of exporter and importer, as controller or processor, determine the modular construction of the contract as described in more detail in the following sections. Clause 2, *effect and invariability of clauses*, specifies the possibility of including the standard contractual clauses within a larger contract and adding additional clauses or guarantees as long as these do not directly or indirectly contradict the standard contractual clauses or infringe upon the fundamental rights and freedoms of data subjects. Clause 3, *third party beneficiaries*, contains the first references to the modular construction of the contract on the basis of the new model contract clauses: depending on the role of exporter and importer, data subjects can invoke and enforce the clauses, as third party beneficiaries, limited to specific clauses. Clause 4, *Interpretation*, refers back to Regulation (EU) 2016/679 for interpretation of the clauses in a sense that is consistent with the rights and obligations under it. Clause 5, *hierarchy*, specifies that in case of contradiction between the standard contractual clauses and the provisions of related agreements in force at the time of acceptance or concluded subsequently, the clauses shall prevail.

The second section, *obligations of the parties*, defines the four possible modular constructions of the contract based on the roles of exporter and importer: module 1 - transfer from controller to controller, module 2 - transfer from controller to processor, module 3 - transfer from controller to processor, module 4 - transfer from controller to processor. The fourth module applies if the controller, established in the European Union, combines data received from the controller, established in the third country, with personal data it has collected in the European Union.

---

[319] Commission Implementing Decision (EU) 2021/914, Article 4, *https://eur-lex.europa.eu/legal-content/IT/TXT/HTML/?uri=CELEX:32021D0914&from=EN#d1e358-31-1* (permanent copy https://perma.cc/L93U-WURX)

To understand the different construction of the contract depending on the form applied, it is useful to refer to some contract clauses of particular interest.

In Module 1, Clause 8, *Data Protection Guarantees*, in paragraph 8.1, *Purpose limitation*, specifies that the importer may process transferred personal data for purposes other than those listed in Annex 1 only if he has obtained the prior consent of the data subject. This paragraph is absent in the other three forms because purpose definition is not part of the controller's duties and is replaced by paragraph 8.1, *instructions*, where, for Modules 2 and 3, the importer undertakes to process personal data only on the documented instructions of the exporter informing him immediately if he is unable to follow those instructions and where, for Module 4, the exporter undertakes to process personal data only on the instructions of the importer informing him if he is unable to follow those instructions, including if those instructions violate Regulation (EU) 2016/679 or other Union or Member State legislation. In Form 1, paragraph 8.5, *security of processing*, specifies that "*the parties shall in particular consider the possibility of using encryption or pseudonymization, including during transmission, if the purpose of the processing can be achieved in this way.*" In Form 2 and 3, in paragraph 8.6, the same sentence continues with the requirement "*in the case of pseudonymization, the additional information for attribution of personal data to a specific data subject shall, where possible, remain under the exclusive control of the exporter.*" Form 1, paragraph 8.7, on *onward transfers,* specifies that the importer is prohibited from disclosing personal data to third parties located outside the European Union, in its own country or in another third country, unless the third party is or agrees to be bound by the same standard contractual clauses, according to the appropriate form. Otherwise, onward transfer is possible only if there is an adequacy decision regarding the third country or with the explicit consent of the data subject. Forms 2 and 3, in Section 8.8, provide for onward transfer only on the documented instruction of the data controller in the European Union.

Clause 10, *Rights of the Data Subject*, specifies how to handle requests for information, rectification, and erasure received from a data subject in relation to the processing of his or her personal data. In Form 1, the importer is required to confirm to the data subject whether or not personal data relating to him or her are being processed, whether they have been or will be subject to onward transfer, to which recipients, and for what purposes, and also rectify inaccurate or incomplete data and erase data relating to the data subject if they are or have been processed in violation of any of the clauses. In Forms 2 and 3, the importer must notify the exporter of requests, without responding directly to the data subject, unless authorized to do so by the data controller in the European Union. In Form 4, the clause specifies that "*the parties should assist each other in responding to inquiries and requests made by data subjects under the local law applicable to the importer or, for data processing by the exporter in the EU, under Regulation (EU) 2016/679.*"

Clause 11, *recourse*, requires the importer to inform interested parties in a transparent and easily accessible form of a contact point authorized to handle complaints by individual notice or on the website. Clause 13, *control*, defines the competent control authority. In the case of an exporter established in a member state of the European Union and or an exporter within the territorial scope of the regulation who has appointed a representative in accordance with Article 27(1) of Regulation (EU) 2016/679, the competent supervisory authority is the one specified in Annex 1 to the standard contractual clauses. In other cases, the competent supervisory authority is that of one of the member states in which the data subjects whose data are transferred under the model contractual clauses are located in connection with the offer of goods or provision of services, or whose conduct is monitored.

The third section, *local legislation and obligations in case of access by public authorities*, is a clear quote to the Schrems II judgment. Clause 14, *Local Legislation and Practices Affecting Compliance with the Clauses*, specifies that "*the parties shall ensure that they have no reason to believe that the legislation and practices of the third country of destination applicable to the importer's processing of personal data, including any personal data disclosure requirements or measures authorizing access by public authorities, prevent the importer from complying with its obligations under these clauses. This is based on the assumption that legislation and practices that respect the essence of fundamental rights and freedoms and do not go beyond what is necessary and proportionate in a democratic society to safeguard one of the objectives set out in Article 23(1) of Regulation (EU) 2016/679 do not contradict these clauses.*" In the case of personal data transfers to the United States of America, the clause requires the implementation of significant technical and organizational measures to ensure confidentiality during the transfer and processing of personal data in the country of destination. Clause 15, Obligations of *the Importer in the Event of Access by Public Authorities*, requires the importer to promptly inform the exporter if it receives a legally binding request from a public authority or becomes aware of any direct access carried out, in accordance with the law of the third country. Where the legislation of the country of destination prevents the importer from informing the exporter or the data subject, the importer nevertheless undertakes to provide as much information as possible regarding the requests received, in particular, regarding the type of data requested and the requesting authorities.

The fourth section, *Final Provisions*, in Clause 16, *Noncompliance with Clauses and Termination*, specifies the suspension of the transfer of personal data to the importer if the importer fails to comply with or violates the standard contractual clauses. The same clause provides for the possibility of each party to revoke its agreement to be bound by the clauses in the event that the European Commission adopts an adequacy decision in relation to the importer's country or in the event that Regulation (EU) 2016/679 becomes part of the legal framework of the destination country. Clause 17, *applicable law*, defines the law of the member state by which the terms of the contract are governed. Clause 18, *choice of court and jurisdiction,* specifies, for forms 1, 2 and 3, the possibility of the data subject to sue the exporter or importer before the courts of a member state while, form 4, defines the country of reference.

The contract includes three annexes. The first annex[320] contains the particulars of the parties: name and address of the company, name, qualification and contact details of the contact person, and an indication of the role as data controller or processor. Following this is a description of the transfer: the categories of data subjects whose personal data are transferred, the categories of personal data transferred, the existence of special data and the safeguards applied taking into account the nature of the data and the risks involved, and the frequency of the transfer. The annex concludes with an indication of the competent supervisory authority in the case of forms 1, 2 and 3.

The second annex[321] , applicable only to forms 1, 2 and 3, details the technical and organizational measures to ensure data security. The explanatory note defines that these should be described in specific, rather than general terms, clearly indicating which measures apply to each transfer. Possible measures include: pseudonymization, encryption of personal data, data minimization, data protection during transmission, data protection during storage, physical security of places where personal data are processed, event logging, and process certification.

---

320 Commission Implementing Decision (EU) 2021/914, Annex I, *https://eur-lex.europa.eu/legal-content/IT/TXT/HTML/?uri=CELEX:32021D0914&from=EN#d1e32-58-1* (permanent copy https://perma.cc/XUU5-S94M)

321 Commission Implementing Decision (EU) 2021/914, Annex II, *https://eur-lex.europa.eu/legal-content/IT/TXT/HTML/?uri=CELEX:32021D0914&from=EN#d1e32-60-1* (permanent copy https://perma.cc/8XCL-QR5R)

The third annex[322] , applicable only to Forms 2 and 3, lists any sub-processors: the name and address of the company, the name, title and contact details of the contact person, and a description of the processing carried out, including a clear delineation of responsibilities if more than one sub-processor is authorized.

[322] Commission Implementing Decision (EU) 2021/914, Annex III, *https://eur-lex.europa.eu/legal-content/IT/TXT/HTML/?uri=CELEX:32021D0914&from=EN#d1e32-61-1* (permanent copy https://perma.cc/T32S-3UZ5)

Chapter 5.
Conclusions

The scope of the second Schrems ruling is not limited to the transfer made by Facebook Ireland Ltd. to Facebook Inc.: a first analysis might lead one to conclude that the companies mainly affected by the declaration of invalidity of the *Privacy Shield* and the new standard contractual clauses are the large U.S. *hi-tech* companies while the impact is even broader and affects almost all EU businesses, from freelancers to large multinationals. To realize this, it is enough to consider that any business nowadays has its own website and that, very often, markers, also known by the term *cookies*, are used to obtain detailed visitor statistics. In the case of *e-commerce* sites, the same technology is used to provide suggestions regarding products on offer or of likely interest to the site visitor.

Among the products used by website creators to obtain this type of information, Google Analytics[323] is used by more than 50 percent of existing websites and has a market share of more than 80 percent when related to the number of visitors[324] . In many other cases, companies' websites use identification and authentication systems based on their users' *social network* profiles, such as Facebook Connect[325] .

Thus, it is easy to imagine the large number of EU companies that, making use of these tools, are affected by the ruling of the Court of Justice of the European Union. Therefore, the one hundred and one complaints[326] filed on August 17, 2020 by the *NOYB* organization against as many European companies found guilty of using Google and Facebook services in the absence of proper disclosure to users even in the absence of an adequacy decision on the protection of personal data exported to the United States of America should come as no surprise.

---

[323] Wikipedia, Google Analytics, *https://it.wikipedia.org/wiki/Google_Analytics* (permanent copy https://perma.cc/6CTE-V5PR)

[324] W3Techs, Usage statistics of traffic analysis tools for websites, *https://w3techs.com/technologies/overview/traffic_analysis* (permanent copy https://perma.cc/3E2T-FQKE)

[325] Wikipedia, Facebook Platform, *https://en.wikipedia.org/wiki/Facebook_Platform* (permanent copy https://perma.cc/CSK5-YKM9)

[326] NOYB, 101 Complaints on EU-US transfers filed, *https://noyb.eu/en/101-complaints-eu-us-transfers-filed* (permanent copy https://perma.cc/H72X-N4C6)

Figure 12 - Symbolic image of the one hundred and one complaints filed by NOYB.[327]

While analyzing the web pages of many European companies, *NOYB* detected code snippets necessary for Google Analytics or Facebook Connect to function despite the ruling of the Court of Justice of the European Union. The allegation made by *NOYB* is the absence of a legal basis authorizing the transfer of data for both companies: Google still claims to rely on the *Privacy Shield* despite its invalidation, Facebook continues to use standard contractual clauses despite the Court's finding that U.S. surveillance laws violate the essence of fundamental rights in the European Union. The one hundred and one complaints were filed in 30 member states of the European Union and the European Economic Area on the basis of the *TLD, top level domain*, of the website: for example, to the Data Protection Authority for all *.it* domains. *NOYB is* asking the data protection authorities to intervene, as provided for in Regulation 2019/679, Article 58, *powers*, and Article 83, *general conditions to impose administrative fines.* Among the companies involved it is interesting to mention the multinationals Airbnb, Auchan, Decathlon, eDreams, Leroy Merlin and the Italian Gruppo Editoriale GEDI[328] , for the *repubblica.it* website, the telephone operator Fastweb[329] and the service *ilmeteo.it*[330] .

---

[327] NOYB, 101 Complaints on EU-US transfers filed, *https://noyb.eu/en/101-complaints-eu-us-transfers-filed* (permanent copy https://perma.cc/H72X-N4C6)

[328] NOYB, Complaint under Articles 77, 80 GDPR against Gedi Gruppo Editoriale and Facebook Ireland Ltd, *https://noyb.eu/files/C29/complaint-30.pdf* (permanent copy https://perma.cc/59J6-8AWB)

[329] NOYB, Complaint under Articles 77, 80 RGPD against Fastweb and Google LLC, *https://noyb.eu/files/C29/complaint-32.pdf*

All complaints have the same structure: the complainant, represented and defended by *NOYB*, files a complaint with the relevant supervisory authority against the domain registrant and the company Google or Facebook reporting the date and time of the visit to the Website. The complaint goes on to allege that "*during the visit to the Website, the owner processed the complainant's personal data (at least his IP address and cookie data)*" while also carrying out its transfer to the U.S. headquarters of Google or Facebook. Such data transfer requires a legal basis under Regulation (EU) 2016/679. Recalling the judgment C-311/18 - Schrems II of the Court of Justice of the European Union that annulled the *Privacy Shield*, the complainant requests that the competent supervisory authority conduct a full investigation of the case, immediately impose the interruption or suspension of any data flow to the U.S. office, and impose an effective, proportionate, and dissuasive financial penalty against the data controller.

One month after the complaints were filed, the reactions are disappointing[331] : only two companies and a university based in the Principality of Liechtenstein contacted *NOYB* and corrected their websites by removing code snippets necessary for Google Analytics or Facebook Connect to work; in all other cases, the complaints were ignored despite possible penalties of up to twenty million euros or 4 percent of annual turnover for a violation of the regulation. In the meantime, the European Data Protection Board has set up a *task force* to deal with the one hundred and one complaints and ensure close cooperation among the board's members: the complaints are essentially identical to each other so if the authority in one member state manages to deal with one in a timely manner, the other authorities must also do the same with mutually consistent outcomes.

The use of Google or Facebook platforms to obtain detailed statistical data is easily overcome as confirmed by the quick resolution of the dispute with the two companies and the Liechtensteinian university also through the use of national and European solutions and products. For example, among the initiatives promoted in recent years by the Digital Italy Agency[332] is a service, currently in *beta*, for the statistical analysis of Italian public

(permanent copy https://perma.cc/T9T5-N2K2)

330 NOYB, Complaint under Articles 77, 80 RGPD against ILMETEO s.r.l. and Google LLC, *https://noyb.eu/files/C29/complaint-33.pdf*
(permanent copy https://perma.cc/6QNJ-QUE2)

331 NOYB, Update on noyb's 101 complaints on EU-US data transfers - only one country shines, *https://noyb.eu/en/update-noybs-101-complaints-eu-us-data-transfers*
(permanent copy *https://perma.cc/6KDR-ZWYQ*)

332 Digital Italy Agency,
https://www.agid.gov.it/
(permanent copy https://perma.cc/557Q-WV7H)

administration websites: Web Analytics Italia[333] . Similarly simple solutions are not available in the case of products related to the monetization of content on the *Web*: the number of global users and the consequent volume of business that can be obtained from global platforms such as Google Ads[334] , formerly Google AdWords, and Meta for Business[335] , formerly known as Facebook for Business, cannot be replicated as effectively through the use of local solutions.

On January 13, 2022, the Austrian authority makes its first partial decision regarding the use of Google Analytics by Verlag GmbH[336] . Despite Google's technical and organizational efforts, such as data encryption and *IP* address pseudonymization, the authority found these measures to be ineffective when it comes to U.S. surveillance. This first decision by a supervisory authority confirms that, in the long run, there may be two options: a major overhaul of U.S. legislation to ensure adequate protection of foreign nationals' personal data to support the U.S. tech industry, or handling foreign nationals' personal data outside the United States. At present, the other regulators have not issued decisions on the other complaints, but it is plausible to expect similar outcomes.

On March 25, 2022, European Commission President Ursula von der Leyen and U.S. President Joe Biden announced an agreement in principle on a new EU-U.S. data sharing system[337] . The agreement, which goes by the name *Trans-Atlantic Data Privacy Framework*[338] , already dubbed by many as *Privacy Shield 2.0*, promises a commitment by the United States of America to implement reforms that will strengthen privacy and civil

---

333 Digital Italy Agency, Web Analytics Italy,
https://webanalytics.italia.it/
(permanent copy https://perma.cc/X96V-B8BN)

334 Wikipedia, Google Ads,
https://it.wikipedia.org/wiki/Google_Ads
(permanent copy https://perma.cc/778X-MDAM)

335 Meta for Business: Marketing on Facebook,
https://www.facebook.com/business
(permanent copy https://perma.cc/T4TV-A6F5)

336 NOYB, Austrian DSB: Use of Google Analytics violates "Schrems II" decision by CJEU,
https://noyb.eu/en/austrian-dsb-eu-us-data-transfers-google-analytics-illegal
(permanent copy https://perma.cc/47TZ-BTLB)

337 European Commission, European Commission and United States Joint Statement on Trans-Atlantic Data Privacy Framework,
https://ec.europa.eu/commission/presscorner/detail/en/IP_22_2087
(permanent copy https://perma.cc/2NF7-24KE)

338 European Commission, Trans-Atlantic Data Privacy Framework,
https://ec.europa.eu/commission/presscorner/api/files/attachment/872132/Trans-Atlantic%20Data%20Privacy%20Framework.pdf
.pdf
(permanent copy https://perma.cc/QT2G-TLPD)

liberties protections applicable to U.S. intelligence activities[339] : new safeguards to ensure predictability and proportionality of surveillance activities for national security purposes, and a new two-tiered independent redress mechanism to implement direct corrective measures and enhance oversight of intelligence activities. The *NOYB* organization's first[340] comment on the announcement is from Max Schrems: "*We already had a purely political agreement in 2015 that had no legal basis. From what we can understand we may be playing the same game a third time. [...] The final text will need more time, once this comes we will analyze it thoroughly, together with our US legal experts. If it is not in line with EU law, we or another group will challenge it. In the end, the Court of Justice will decide a third time. [...] It is regrettable that the European Union and the United States of America have not used this situation to come to a "no spy" agreement with basic guarantees between like-minded democracies. Customers and businesses will face another few years of* legal *uncertainty.*"[341] .

---

339 The White House, United States and European Commission Announce Trans-Atlantic Data Privacy Framework,
https://www.whitehouse.gov/briefing-room/statements-releases/2022/03/25/fact-sheet-united-states-and-european-commission-announce-trans-atlantic-data-privacy-framework/
(permanent copy *https://perma.cc/LTQ2-VQ3D*)

340 NOYB, "Privacy Shield 2.0?" - First Reaction by Max Schrems,
https://noyb.eu/en/privacy-shield-20-first-reaction-max-schrems
(permanent copy https://perma.cc/9S3F-XMKU)

341 We already had a purely political deal in 2015 that had no legal basis. From what you hear we could play the same game a third time now. The deal was apparently a symbol that von der Leyen wanted, but does not have support among experts in Brussels, as the US did not move. It is especially appalling that the US has allegedly used the war on Ukraine to push the EU on this economic matter.

The final text will need more time, once this arrives we will analyze it in depth, together with our US legal experts. If it is not in line with EU law, we or another group will likely challenge it. In the end, the Court of Justice will decide a third time. We expect this to be back at the Court within months from a final decision.

It is regrettable that the EU and US have not used this situation to come to a 'no spy' agreement, with baseline guarantees among like-minded democracies. Customers and businesses face more years of legal uncertainty.

Bibliography and references

Charter of Fundamental Rights of the European Union, Charter of Nice

https://www.europarl.europa.eu/charter/pdf/text_it.pdf
(permanent copy https://perma.cc/E4QG-VVMB)

Clarifying Lawful Overseas Use of Data Act

https://www.congress.gov/bill/115th-congress/senate-bill/2383/text
(permanent copy https://perma.cc/DM5E-TCBS)

European Commission

https://ec.europa.eu/info/index_it
(permanent copy https://perma.cc/V8AC-9W45)

Convention 108 of the Council of Europe, Strasbourg Convention, Convention for the Protection of Individuals with regard to Automatic Processing of Personal Data

https://rm.coe.int/1680078c45
(permanent copy https://perma.cc/28Z5-XX3J)

European Convention on Human Rights

https://www.echr.coe.int/Documents/Convention_ITA.pdf
(permanent copy https://perma.cc/KXB9-QRAG)

Court of Justice of the European Union

https://curia.europa.eu/jcms/jcms/j_6/it/
(permanent copy https://perma.cc/WG7J-W84S)

Commission Decision 2000/520/EC of July 26, 2000, pursuant to Directive 95/46/EC of the European Parliament and of the Council on the adequacy of the protection afforded by the Safe Harbor Principles and related "Frequently Asked Questions" (FAQs) on privacy published by the U.S. Department of Commerce

https://eur-lex.europa.eu/legal-content/IT/TXT/?uri=CELEX:32000D0520
(permanent copy https://perma.cc/UX7L-XACB)

Commission Decision 2010/87/EU of 5 February 2010 on standard contractual clauses for the transfer of personal data to processors established in third countries under Directive 95/46/EC of the European Parliament and of the Council

https://eur-lex.europa.eu/legal-content/IT/TXT/?uri=CELEX:32010D0087
(permanent copy https://perma.cc/3NWA-4426)

Commission Implementing Decision (EU) 2016/1250 of July 12, 2016, pursuant to Directive 95/46/EC of the European Parliament and of the Council, on the adequacy of the protection provided by the EU-US privacy shield regime

https://eur-lex.europa.eu/legal-content/IT/TXT/?uri=CELEX%3A32016D1250
(permanent copy https://perma.cc/8YLX-LC26)

Commission Implementing Decision (EU) 2021/914 of 4 June 2021 on standard contractual clauses for the transfer of personal data to third countries under Regulation (EU) 2016/679 of the European Parliament and of the Council

https://eur-lex.europa.eu/legal-content/IT/TXT/HTML/?uri=CELEX:32021D0914
(permanent copy https://perma.cc/T986-DUY8)

Legislative Decree No. 196 of June 30, 2003, "Code for the Protection of Personal Data"

https://web.camera.it/parlam/leggi/deleghe/testi/03196dl.htm
(permanent copy https://perma.cc/74UQ-VGGG)

Legislative Decree No. 69 of May 28, 2012, "Amendments to Legislative Decree No. 196 of June 30, 2003, containing the Personal Data Protection Code in implementation of Directives 2009/136/EC on the processing of personal data and the protection of privacy in the electronic communications sector and 2009/140/EC on electronic communications networks and services and Regulation (EC) No. 2006/2004 on cooperation between national authorities responsible for the enforcement of consumer protection laws"

https://www.gazzettaufficiale.it/eli/id/2012/05/31/012G0090/sg
(permanent copy https://perma.cc/26K4-PD7L)

Directive 95/46/EC of the European Parliament and of the Council of 24 October 1995 on the protection of individuals with regard to the processing of personal data and on the free movement of such data

https://eur-lex.europa.eu/legal-content/IT/ALL/?uri=CELEX:31995L0046
(permanent copy https://perma.cc/MD4V-TPV5)

Directive 97/66/EC of the European Parliament and of the Council of 15 December 1997 concerning the processing of personal data and the protection of privacy in the telecommunications sector

https://eur-lex.europa.eu/legal-content/IT/TXT/?uri=CELEX%3A31997L0066
(permanent copy https://perma.cc/U9CW-ARFS)

Directive 2002/58/EC of the European Parliament and of the Council of 12 July 2002 concerning the processing of personal data and the protection of privacy in the electronic communications sector (Directive on privacy and electronic communications)

https://eur-lex.europa.eu/legal-content/IT/ALL/?uri=CELEX:32002L0058
(permanent copy https://perma.cc/43PE-BTSX)

Directive 2006/24/EC of the European Parliament and of the Council of 15 March 2006 on the retention of data generated or processed in connection with the provision of publicly available electronic communications services or of public communications networks and amending Directive 2002/58/EC

https://eur-lex.europa.eu/legal-content/IT/TXT/?uri=celex:32006L0024
(permanent copy https://perma.cc/HWK6-FYKT)

Directive 2009/136/EC of the European Parliament and of the Council of November 25, 2009 amending Directive 2002/22/EC on universal service and users' rights relating to electronic communications networks and services, Directive 2002/58/EC concerning the processing of personal data and the protection of privacy in the electronic communications sector and Regulation (EC) No. 2006/2004 on cooperation between national authorities responsible for the enforcement of consumer protection laws

https://eur-lex.europa.eu/legal-content/IT/TXT/?uri=CELEX:32009L0136
(permanent copy https://perma.cc/NQY6-6H5C)

Europe v. Facebook

http://www.europe-v-facebook.org/EN/en.html
(permanent copy https://perma.cc/33BU-TERE)

Executive Order 12333 of the President of the United States of America.

https://irp.fas.org/offdocs/eo/eo-13470.htm
(permanent copy https://perma.cc/Y6HF-XB7B)

Export.gov

https://2016.export.gov/
(permanent copy https://perma.cc/22GQ-5DTS)

Data Protection Authority

https://www.garanteprivacy.it/
(permanent copy https://perma.cc/39VD-YCEA)

Law No. 675 of December 31, 1996, "Protection of persons and other subjects with regard to the processing of personal data"

https://parlamento.it/parlam/leggi/96675l.htm
(permanent copy https://perma.cc/P8DR-PPBU)

NOYB - European Center for Digital Rights

https://noyb.eu/en
(permanent copy https://perma.cc/92E4-25T5)

Privacy Shield Framework

https://www.privacyshield.gov/
(permanent copy https://perma.cc/K87Z-LYMX)

Fourth Amendment of the Constitution of the United States of America.

https://constitution.congress.gov/constitution/amendment-4/
(permanent copy https://perma.cc/6YGT-N3GP)

Regulation (EU) 2016/679 of the European Parliament and of the Council of 27 April 2016 on the protection of individuals with regard to the processing of personal data and on the free movement of such data and repealing Directive 95/46/EC (General Data Protection Regulation)

https://eur-lex.europa.eu/legal-content/IT/TXT/?uri=CELEX:32016R0679
(permanent copy https://perma.cc/UB9M-KSHU)

Treaty on the Functioning of the European Union

https://eur-lex.europa.eu/legal-content/IT/TXT/?uri=CELEX:12012E/TXT
(permanent copy https://perma.cc/A8NQ-AHYY)

Printed by Books on Demand GmbH, Norderstedt / Germany